Be Intentional Culture

How the Small Things Enhance or Undermine Your Culture

Introduction by Michelle Blevins

Authors:
Luke Draeger
Lisa Lavender
Andrew G. McCabe
Dr. Leroy Nunery II
David Princeton
Elan Pasmanick
Jonathan L. Isaacson
Chris Stanley
Jeremy Watkin

Editing by Jon Isaacson and Tiffany Acuff

Published by The DYOJO

Bill —
I know you have worked to raise the bar for the industry & contribute to strong cultures, looking forward to your feedback. Keep doing good things!

INTRODUCTION

By Michelle Blevins

*"You are your culture. Culture is a reflection of
who you are and what you do as a team."*
- Jon Isaacson, The Intentional Restorer

It is a tale as old as time.

It was all going so well.

Or so they thought.

ABC Restoration lived by the phrase "because we've always done it that way." And while profitability wasn't necessarily soaring year-over-year, things were steady. Senior management came and went as they pleased (that's the goal of ownership, right?!); doing what was necessary to keep the business operating at status quo. A high rate of technician turnover continued too, but that was totally normal.

Don't all insurance damage restoration companies have that? The company wined and dined the right people, sponsored golf outings for their sales team, and had a fancy logo that carried across their fleet, polos, and even coffee mugs. They were known for their logo, but not much else.

Then, the owner passed away. And new ownership came in. They rejected the status quo; they wanted a business that grows and thrives, and a team with hearts and drive to match.

After years of little innovation or change, the other shoe had dropped.

Within a few months, the new owner had made some good changes to project workflow and made some key hires; people who also wanted to be part of a healthy, growing company and team. While a select few star players from the "old regime" connected with the new leadership, others insisted they continue doing things "the way we've always done it." After all, if it isn't broke, don't fix it!

But in 2020, simply maintaining the status quo as a restoration company will not keep you relevant nor profitable. You must be a constant driver of change.

The new ownership of ABC Restoration started to change the culture from the inside, out. As new technology was brought in, some estimators and project managers refused to learn and evolve. One was a steady producer for the company, and well-liked by customers, but was also heard speaking against the new leadership as changes were implemented and created an overall atmosphere of negativity in the production department.

The office manager had a similar story. Daily conversations sounded something like … "Why change collection practices if we don't have to? 90-day turnaround for payment was always fine before! Why implement this new job management software when files work perfectly well? No, that customer is being difficult and not worth my time to talk to. You handle her, Karen."

The negativity from key players in the "old regime" was toxic to the company's culture; stifling the entire team as a whole, no matter how much others tried to stay positive and press forward. It didn't take long for negative players to be shown the door, or find their own way out.

Andy McCabe delivers a very simple fact in his chapter of this book: "I've never fired someone too soon."

Within nine months, the entire feeling inside ABC Restoration had changed. New technology was helping streamline jobs considerably, meaning fewer change orders and customers who could see where projects were at right within an app. Jobs were being paid much sooner. Overall, operations were trending in a more positive direction, and the company was on track to be up 10% in revenue for the year, with even bigger projections further into the future.

But all that wasn't the biggest change. The biggest change came in the culture of the company.

After months of discomfort, things had turned a corner - and employees smiled every morning when they walked through the door. Wins were celebrated; people were "caught doing good"; and most of all, every job became a true team effort.

Everyone realized without the techs crawling in spider-filled crawl spaces, there would be no work! Likewise, everyone realized without a project coordinator keeping software files updated and staying on top of project manager and estimator tasks, jobs wouldn't be running as smoothly.

Every single person was important to the completion of the job.

Everyone worked the on-call rotation.

Everyone spoke with customers.

Everyone lived with customer service top-of-mind.

Culture is Critical

I remember a few years ago when talking about millennials in the workforce was the big thing. Today, it is all about culture. Companies that simply maintain the status quo will not last.

This brilliant book, brought together by some forward-thinking leaders in the restoration and insurance world, offers chapter-by-chapter wisdom and guidance on fostering a culture that is healthy on the inside, and shines vibrantly on the exterior of everyone associated with your company.

Jon Isaacson nails the importance of a healthy company culture right off the bat...

> "A solid culture is essential for remaining competitive in the current marketplace and will continue to grow in prominence as the speed of change accelerates in the coming years."

As Jeremy Watkins drives home in his chapter, it all starts with you, the leader. He drives home four core lessons on company culture...

Lesson 1: Don't preach it until you practice it yourself.

Lesson 2: Admit when your works and actions are incongruent.

Lesson 3: Integrity is everything.

Lesson 4: Stop passing the buck.

"Put simply," Jeremy writes, "This shift to practicing what I preach has been life changing for me as a manager, customer service professional, and human being."

Wisdom + Experience + Leadership

Every single chapter of this book is packed full of life and career experiences, and wisdom. While I don't have the pleasure of knowing each author personally, I do know about half of them, and let you tell you – they are dynamite!

As you read this, you will glean some amazing nuggets of wisdom to take into your own company, and also find many of the stories relatable – both on the topic of company culture, and also on leadership.

These writers are not preaching at you; they are here to lift you up! They are real leaders just like you.

Check out Andy's chapter. Have you ever had an employee steal from you? Andy talks about what happened, the implications of a star player with questionable ethics, and how culture could foster repeated negative behavior.

Ever had an employee who you just know could be a key player in your organization, but you've tried (what you think is) everything and there's been no change? Author Luke Draeger can relate! He tried to train Diane to rock sales without success, until...

> "...a miracle happened—not a grandiose parting of the Red Sea type of miracle, but the small, every day sort we tend to take for granted. A child's first words might be a proper comparison, only Diane wasn't the one who needed to learn to speak better; I was. I needed to learn to speak Diane's language."

As a leader, do you speak the language of those on your team? Everyone speaks a little differently! Effective leaders of healthy companies understand and embrace the uniqueness of each member of the team!

Lisa Lavender speaks to a very simple, but perhaps one of the most vital components of leadership and development of a healthy company culture. It's SO important, she calls it "super fuel."

Any guesses what it is?

It's saying "thank you." Simple as that.

Even lacking something this small can have a huge impact on your company.

When was the last time you said "thank you"?

Learn from Mistakes

If you're overwhelmed with the state of your company, and you're grabbing this book hoping for some wisdom, take heart – it's here! You know what's also here? The approval to make mistakes – as long as you learn from them!

David Princeton shares his journey to law school within this book, and admits to his mistakes, and also speaks to the value of surrounding yourself by the right people.

> *"Mistakes. Along the way I will make mistakes. Lots of mistakes. But that is one of the beautiful things about life, learning from those mistakes. I now make it a point to share my mistakes with others, hoping that expressing a vulnerability will empower them to make a better decision than I made. Everyone's experience is uniquely their own and sharing that experience can lead to some incredible things!"*

Again, developing a healthy company culture, and life relationships, starts with you. Take ownership for your behavior, your leadership.

If you've read all the way to here, kudos – you'll for sure make it through the entire book if you could listen to me for this long!

Here's my final sales point, if you need it. If you love Doritos, this book is for you. Only Jon could effectively weave a Doritos analogy into a book on company culture.

In Jon's words, *keep doing good things*.

FOREWARD

A Tumultuous Process

This was supposed to be my first book. Selfishly, I thought that if I wrote a collaborative book, I could help myself both refine my writing process as well as expand my network of influence by tapping into the networks of my co-authors. Of course, this would be a win-win as they would all cumulatively benefit from the expansion as well.

A few setbacks befell us, even prior to the onset of COVID-19. Many of the initial contributors had to peel off of the project as their workload increased in late 2019 and early 2020. You will remember, the twentieth year of the two thousands started off with plenty of issues sans the pandemic. As people were navigating those concerns, this book became an item that could logically be removed to lessen the strain on contributor's physical, mental, and emotional capacity.

Our publisher, which had experience in all of the areas that I did not, also had some disruption that required their immediate attention, and they too had to recuse themselves from the then unnamed collaborative work. At that point, I didn't think it was fair to have my first self publishing venture be one that could negatively impact what remained of my co-author troupe. Not that I wouldn't give the project my 100% effort, but I didn't know what I didn't know and would be learning the process from scratch.

So, I decided to pause this book on culture and focus my efforts on teaching myself to publish using my first solo project, *Be Intentional: Estimating*, as the guinea pig. This first book, by many accounts, is much more tactical. It is industry specific to property restoration, even though I attempt to demonstrate that one of the tools for estimating, Xactimate, can have some useful applications to contractors who aren't already using a standardized estimating tool. I discussed with Mark Springer, owner of Dayspring Restoration, on the DYOJO Podcast Episode 41, how I view estimating as a component of the culture in the construction industry. In my estimating book, I discuss how status quo mindsets and habits negatively impact the people, process, production, and progress of an organization.

We know bad culture when we see it, yet it may not always lend itself to clear definitions. One common factor in the mindset and habits that lead to enhancing your culture is this:

> Taking care of your culture is critical to taking care of your people.
> Taking care of your people is essential to taking care of your customers.
>
> Taking care of your customers is the foundation of a sustainable business.

Therefore, developing, adapting, and caring for your culture is vital to your vitality as an organization. Your input of time, effort, and resources towards developing an intentional culture is directly linked to achieving optimal business outputs.

I hope that this book has been structured to be a cohesive read through as well as something that will be a reference resource when you need some inspiration as you work to build your team and culture. In the author bio section we have included contact information and relevant websites for our group so that you can follow them and reach out if needed. I have known many of the authors through social media and industry involvement, and have been happy to get to know many of them more deeply as we worked through this writing process. You will note that many of the co-authors have been guests on my podcast as I have learned a lot from each of them and want the world to hear their great insights on mindset and habits leading to enhancing strong cultures.

As we continue to dig into this subject matter, the question we are asking is:
What are some of the small things that have helped to enhance, or undermine, culture in the experiences of our talented group of authors?

As a sidenote, I think you will find this book has a bit more grammatical polish thanks to the careful editing eye of Tiffany Acuff.

CHAPTER 1

What is Culture and Why Should I Care?

Encouragement for People in a Position of Leadership

By Jon Isaacson

T *the art of yelling.* Culture has been a buzzword for sometime in the wide world of business. Like most jargon, you may be asking whether culture has any real value when it comes to producing results in your business. My hope is that this book will help provide you with actionable insights (to borrow a phrase from the restoration industry educators by the same name) from real people who are fighting the good fight of trying to develop themselves and their businesses the right way.

I was trying to remember when I first heard about or consciously experienced culture in the workplace. *It started with a yell.*

Do you remember the first time you were yelled at in the workplace?

Can you bring yourself back to that time, the preceding events and your feelings in that moment?

Before we get into my story, I believe there is an art to yelling. If you disagree, you might at least concede that there is a nuance to yelling. Agreed?

Well, if you do agree, then you also know that nuance is a component of art.

Ergo, there is an art to yelling.

Therefore, I win.

So, because I won that argument rather deftly, I will further postulate that if there is an art to yelling, then conversely there has to be an art to being yelled at. Which we will explore further in the next chapter.

When I say that there is an art to yelling, I don't want the reader to think that yelling is art. What I am addressing is the broader aspect of *correction*. There is definitely an art to correction. While you may not need to yell in order to correct, you cannot get around the need to correct if you are hiring, training and developing a strong culture.

If the goal of art is to communicate a message or a feeling, as people in a position of leadership we must learn to develop our abilities to understand and work with our mediums for improvement effectively. Managers have a variety of tools at their disposal, and as was stated, by Mark Cornelius in my first book, "Learn how to use the hammer [tool] to its utmost capabilities. Become the most proficient person on the planet with that hammer [tool]."[1]

While this chapter uses yelling as the medium, remember we are discussing correction as it relates to culture. If you are going to improve your culture, you must discipline *your* self, *your* mindset and *your* habits, before you can correct your team and affect the progress of your organization.

Yelling varies by pitch, volume and intensity (elements of art). For example, a low intensity, high pitch and high volume yell isn't as emotionally jarring as a high intensity, low pitch and high volume yell. As you implement your efforts to correct and improve your culture, you must constantly be asking yourself whether your methods are producing the results that you seek.

This can be deceptive. For example, when you yell, your team members may snap to attention but is that modus operandi producing sustainable results? Developing a culture means you are building clarity, consistency and accountability so that the mechanism for improvement is internal rather than requiring you to constantly be present to ameliorate.

I want to assure the reader that I believe there is a line, that yelling should not be your default, nor should it be the norm. In a book about culture, I will say definitively that if you are a person in a position of leadership and you are constantly losing your cool, you have a problem. If your organizational habits acquiesce to chaos as normative then your culture is broken. Your yells will produce short term results, but if yelling has been your only correctional tool it is time to add some gadgets to your arsenal.

When you are faced with dysfunction you must trace it to its roots. Often the answers are closer than we want to admit. Before you go about your business of blaming everyone else for the issues that set you off, it would benefit all parties for those in a position of leadership to address their own shortcomings first.

Skylar Lewis, CEO of Superior Restoration in Lake Elsinore, California, joined us for a candid conversation on The DYOJO Podcast[2] where he shared his experience with the value of facing the fact that he needed to change before his company could grow. This process enabled him to own the issues in his organization, to see himself as the common denominator, to address his dysfunctional culture and work to filter clarity through the organization.

As we consider culture, improvement, correction and even yelling, I would like it to also be stated, for the record, that humans make mistakes. Even good managers have their moments of weakness.

Back to the yell that may have started it all.

I can recall being yelled at early in my professional development. In fact, it was so early in the professional portion of my development that it wasn't in the formal sequence of my career. Shall we say it was developmental but it was not yet professional. I was around 12 years old and I was building a deck with my uncle who was a contractor.

To provide some of the back story, I often went to my aunt and uncle's home over periods of my summer break. My cousin and I enjoyed visiting job sites where my uncle was engaged in constructing various homes throughout Western Washington. As we grew older we were given opportunities to assist with relatively menial tasks such as sweeping out houses or picking up debris from the various skilled trades.

You could imagine that the invitation to assist with building a deck came with some exuberance on our part. We were finally getting the chance to help with something important. Our work would now have a higher purpose.

As I discussed with Shannon Tymosko, an up and coming tradesperson and ambassador for Kickass Careers, on The DYOJO Podcast,[3] in the skilled trades, one of the great joys is being able to stand back and see the fruits of your labor. She shared a story about unlocking her passion for construction when her friend invited her to assist with a kitchen remodel.

For many young people who are still searching for a career path, an introduction to that feeling of crafting something with your own hands can be the spark that gets the motivational fire burning. As such, managers should resist the temptation to pass on candidates based upon tired metrics such as "career hopping" or short term employment history.

For my cousin and I, the opportunity to put our mark in the contracting world as having helped with building a deck was a next level accomplishment. From this day forward the world would know that we had a part in building this deck - or at least that is how we viewed it.

As we prepared for the work to commence my uncle gave us an overview of what we would be doing. He briefed us on the safety precautions and ran us through how to operate the necessary tools. I don't remember how much we actually helped with the building of the deck but I do recall that we were helping him to screw down the deck boards.

The work progressed into a system of bringing in materials, preparing an area, supplying my uncle with screws and moving the tools down to the next row. Our job was to keep the machine running smoothly.

Whatever you are involved in, the basic tasks are often the most critical to success. As people in a position of leadership we must be able to communicate and train our team members to **Do It Right**. This is the foundation of a strong and sustainable culture. A team that does it right consistently will have a shot at being competitive over the long haul.

While my cousin and I had a system going, we started waining in our concentration and our progress suffered. We were warned. We regained momentum. Inevitably the cycle repeated. Then it came - the low pitch, high volume and high intensity yell.

We had crossed the line.

We lost concentration, we were negatively impacting production and we needed to get back on track.

My uncle yelled something to the effect of, "We have been doing the same task all day, *why don't I have any screws in my hand?*" It was not a pleasant exchange but from my recollection we were able to complete the project without getting yelled at again - for that day.

I think it is vital that those in a position of leadership, especially in the skilled trades and service based businesses, understand that we don't want to tell our team members to do it faster. Faster usually comes at the cost of quality. My uncle was not upset because he had an unrealistic expectation of our production capabilities (a common pitfall for status quo managers), he was angry that we weren't maintaining our responsibility to the process.

Once our team members understand how to Do It Right, we want to teach them how to **Do It Efficiently**. Efficiency has as much to do with reducing waste as it does with increasing value. On that deck, we needed to operate as a three person team keeping the process operating as efficiently as possible to keep our skilled laborer stocked so that he could keep laying boards.

In property restoration, if our team members are going to their vehicle we want them carrying something (I.E. bags of debris) and if they are returning to the worksite they need to be carrying something (I.E. tools, equipment). In remodeling, we constantly hear business owners lament the unnecessary trips to the hardware store by their carpenters. In carpet cleaning it's similar to restoration - no wasted trips back and/or forth. On larger construction projects, when the plan isn't thought through or executed, standby time can be very costly.

Emotional Credits Before Emotional Debits

For those entering the workforce, I believe it is important to understand that yelling has some nuance to it. There are different types of yelling and there are different causes for these outbursts. For those in a position of leadership, it is important to remember that no one grew up the way you did, had the same work experiences you did and they don't view the world in general the same way you do.

Managers are unique.

Employees are unique.

We are all human.

That day on that deck, we had been instructed, trained and even demonstrated periods of success (we were capable). If we were going to be victorious as a team, my cousin and I needed to focus our attention and effort. We were padawans and needed to learn from a jedi if we wanted to continue our pursuit of building bigger and better things. The "yell" from that day left an indelible mark in my life and was one of many important lessons along the way of my professional development.

I knew that my uncle loved me even if he yelled at me. I wanted to be there and I wanted to learn. At work love may be a bit strong. But, like my uncle, those in a position of leadership need to understand that in many ways people are like banks - you have to make emotional deposits (credits) if you want to effectively make emotional withdrawals (debits). This instance of correction by my uncle was deserved and had been supported by many positive emotional deposits.

I am not talking about manipulation. I am talking about human interaction. As a person in a position of leadership, you often have to address issues in your organization (correction). Again, I don't believe that yelling should be the default or even the norm. It's probably odd to open a book about culture with a story about yelling. But if you have been following anything The DYOJO does, you know that we like to swim against the current.

My point here is that clarity and consistency lead to accountability. Before you can build or expect accountability in your culture, you must build a foundation of clarity and consistency. In doing so you must teach your team how to Do It Right. As they learn to consistently operate with integrity you want to teach them to Do It Efficiently. Train your team how to increase value while reducing waste.

Be clear and teach your team to *do it right.*

Build consistency and help your team to *do it efficiently.*

Develop accountability and show your team how to *do it excellently.*

Accountability and Excellence

The final goal is to empower your team members to **Do It Excellently**. If you want your organization to be known for excellency, you must first teach your team members to do things right and to be efficient.

As a dedicated carpenter, my uncle demonstrated that the key to doing it excellently meant first, doing it right. You cannot be excellent if you don't even know how to do it right. Construction is both art and science. Those that can meld the two are master craftsmen. In property restoration I call them Doctors of Disaster.

My uncle was a stickler for doing things the right way but he also found simple ways to dress things up with unique features. One of his trademarks was a sunburst pattern on the gable of the garage. Many of the homes he built still bear this simple but elegant touch of pzazz.

Most managers want accountability but are not disciplined themselves in communicating clearly or building consistency. Yelling is not the most effective form of communication available to people in a position of leadership as it originates from a lack of control and often makes a deep draw on emotional currency. That said, even good people make mistakes and there are times when a yell may be the element needed for a breakthrough.

In his book, *Joy, Inc.: How We Built a Workplace People Love*, author Richard Sheridan reflects on the mindset and habits of a manager that will help their intentional culture at Menlo thrive. After outlining a scenario where the team had to work together to identify shortfalls and source solutions, he states that culture enhancing managers, "Exercise emotional control and allow those they are leading to make mistakes while ensuring they don't flounder."[4]

Being a person in a position of leadership is not easy but it doesn't have to be overly complex. Leading yourself often requires keeping things simple. Leading others is often a process of making what seems to be difficult simple for those you are helping (simplify the concepts). Developing your culture comes down to those decisions that either *enhance* what you are building or *undermine* what you have been saying.

> <u>People in a position of leadership are responsible for:</u>
> Clarity
> Consistency
> Accountability
>
> <u>Team members must learn to:</u>
> Do It Right
> Do It Efficiently
> Do It Excellently

If you are a person in a position of leadership and you are frustrated with your people, start by asking whether you have done your part to communicate clearly and develop consistency. Before you yell, ask your team members whether you have been unclear about a step in the process and work together to fix both the errors from the employee and the ineffective means of communication on your part.

> "On our team we expect you to Do It Right. We are going to train you to Do It Right by showing you how to Do It Right. Once you have mastered this you will be a part of our culture of helping and holding ALL team members to this standard.
>
> If at any point you are not clear on how to Do It Right, please ask so that we can help you. If you get it wrong, we will help you. If you do it wrong we will work to find ways to be more effective in our training.
>
> If you consistently do it wrong we may have to determine whether you are unwilling or incapable of learning to Do It Right, we will see if there is a better fit for you elsewhere in our company or perhaps in another organization."

Making a commitment to your culture does not mean that you do not uphold a standard. Culture is the dedication to clarity and consistency so that accountability flows from within the organization. As Klark Brown from The Alliance of Independent Restorers (AIR) says, "Coach them up or coach them out." The goal is to recruit, hire, train and develop in accordance with culture so that we are not wasting our energy with dysfunction.

CHAPTER 2

What is Culture and Why Should I Care?

Encouragement for Growth Minded Professionals

By Jon Isaacson

T*he art of being yelled at.* In life you will face failures and setbacks; these are not the end of the road. You need to know this as a growth minded professional. You will have to endure correction, discipline and likely even some yelling in order to achieve upward mobility in a career path that you find rewarding. You will have to weigh whether the experience is worth the payout. As described in my prior chapter, The Art of Yelling, I am thankful that my cousin and I weren't yelled at all the time as we learned the basics of the skilled trades; nor were we yelled at out of pure vitriol.

If you were not exposed to the art of yelling, or shall we say the proper execution of correction, outbursts of emotion in the workplace may shock you. So, how then do you develop the art of being yelled at? How do you respond properly to correction even if your discipline is unfairly administered?

My father-in-law has taught many people how to lead by learning first how to be a good follower. He has an acronym that those who have learned under him know quite well. He will put his massive hand on your shoulder, stare directly into your

eyes and tell you that you need to be, "F-A-T." This is a helpful framework both for those learning to excel within a culture
and will help managers to more effectively communicate with
their team members.

F = Be Faithful.

We hear often that modern workers want to do work that is
meaningful. I don't disagree, but I also don't see this as being
unique to any generation, as I have met only a handful of people
of any age that didn't care whether their work had any purpose.
If you want to grow in your professional development, you
must learn to grind through those things that you may perceive
as mundane so that you can learn to do things of greater intri-
cacy, purpose and value.

I wrote an article for Insurance Nerds which took a look at *The
Four Keys to Developing a Well-Rounded Growth Mindset*[5] by digging into a speech from 1967 given by Martin Luther King Jr to a
group of junior high students. Dr. King's speech was titled *What
Is Your Life's Blueprint?*

> *The cult of success causes us to idolize the achievers who
> are most apparent in movies, business and who have attained
> affluence. If the vision of your blueprint is to build a purpose-
> ful and happy existence then the result of our life's work is not
> guaranteed to bring those physical rewards. Dr. King admon-
> ished the students, "If it falls to your lot to be a street sweeper,
> sweep streets so well that all the hosts of heaven and earth will
> have to pause and say: Here lived a great street sweeper who
> swept his job well."*

Wherever you are, you must be faithful to perform the roles
and responsibilities of your current position to the best of your
abilities if you want to unlock opportunities for advancement.
As Dr. King states, whatever your task is, "Do it so well that all
the hosts of heaven and earth will have to pause and say: Here
lived a great _____ (fill in the blank with what your role is)
who _____ his (or her) job well." This applies to all workers at

all levels in all organizations.

Another pivotal character at the nexus of human history and doing things the right way put it this way, "He who is faithful in little will be faithful in much."[6] With both admonitions, the formula for demonstrating that you can take on more responsibility is first by first proving that you can kick butt (Do it Right, Efficiently and Excellently) in your current role, regardless of how mundane it may seem.

As a person in a position of leadership you must have some view of the bigger picture if you are going to lead your team to achieve your shared goals. Before you can ask people to follow you, you must be equally invested in becoming a person who inspires others to follow rather than relying on the requirement to do so. Being a manager demands that you constantly learn how to adapt so that you can effectively communicate a vision worth fighting for.

If you want to be a high flyer, you must Inspire more than you require.

A = Be Available.

There may be a day where you really messed up and you received a harsh butt chewing. Whether it's the mistake that you made or the response that you received or the combination of both, you will question whether you want to go back. You have to decide what is best for you but often you can build more respect for yourself and from others by coming back from a defeat than by walking away from it. Even if it's justified, giving up rarely leads to a positive long term outcome. How you respond to mistakes as an individual is a defining moment for yourself.

Being available, first and foremost, means showing up and doing what you said you would do. It is amazing how many people say they want a job, book an interview and then don't show up - no call, no text. It is even more perplexing when a manager gives someone a chance, especially someone who begged for the job, and within a few weeks they are showing up late, or no call - no show, to work. Being available, showing up, will open you to a world of opportunities.

Before you can even Do It Right, you must show up to be able to do it *at all*.

How you deal with mistakes is also a defining moment in your culture. Errors should not be glossed over, but you must have a process for enabling your team to make honest mistakes. In my experience you will gain a lot more engagement by viewing incidents where the team missed the mark as teaching moments as opposed to blowing people up. We will share examples of what not to do, as often that is how we learn when we are in positions of leadership, including a story from my past when I discovered *The Naughty Board* (dun-dun-duh).

Being available as a person in a position of leadership means being open to feedback and getting to know your team so that you can communicate with them on a personal level.

T = Be Teachable.

As an employee with a growth mindset, your professional development will bring you into contact with various leadership styles. There are those managers who will teach you what to do by their positive and effective example. Conversely, there are those people in a position of leadership who will teach you what not to do by their negative or ineffective example. As well, there will be plenty of supervisors who are a bit of both; they will have a few strengths and some glaring weaknesses.

I addressed some of this in my book *Be Intentional: Estimating*[7] where I addressed the "David's" in most organizations. A David is someone who:

> Puts the team first
> Is a grinder (hardworking)
> Learns to do things the right way
> Works diligently at being efficient

Seeks to add a touch of excellence to everything they do
Often is overlooked by their bosses

My encouragement to you, especially if you are a *David* is to recognize and learn to play *the game*. If you aren't getting the advancement opportunities that you seek, "Make a few small changes to play the game better without compromising your values. Think through what it would look like to position yourself to change the current perception of your value." If you have done everything that you can to demonstrate your value and play the game, it may be time to explore possibilities in the open market.

Remember, life is about opportunity NOT convenience. Do the best you can to identify and make the most of your current opportunities.

If you want to grow you will have to be stretched, tested and broken in order to raise your ceiling. You are in the driver seat of your destiny and every decision has consequences. Rather than steer away from hard lessons, lean into them and emerge a better person. *Not all people in a position of leadership know how to teach, but they can all teach you something.*

If you are a person in a position of leadership, you will need to recognize the importance of being intentional in developing yourself and your culture. The good news is that it is not as complicated as many make it. I hope you will see that this book is not about jargon, but real world examples of real people sharing their experiences with how small things can lead to big results. We will cover many of the principles that my talented guests on The DYOJO Podcast share about the lessons they have learned as they have built their careers and their organizations.

My fellow authors and I want to help you shorten your DANG learning curve as you develop your culture.

The best way to foster a teachable culture is for those in a position of leadership to invest in professional development for themselves (lead by example) and for their team members (lead with opportunity). Remember, in order for these training mediums to be engaging there needs to be practical application to the existing work as well as the pathway to real growth. *Inspire more than you require.*

Your principles as a manager shouldn't change but your mechanisms will need to be updated. Tony Canas and Carly Burnham have written an excellent book for anyone struggling to connect with the current workforce; *Insuring Tomorrow* is a textbook for *engaging millennials.* They share a story (page 85) where an interviewee arrived late, was underdressed for the occasion and bombed the interview. Rather than assume the worst, the hiring manager advised the candidate on how to make a better showing for the process and gave them a second chance.

This young person did as they were instructed and turned out to be a good hire. When we don't update our perspectives as people in a position of leadership, we miss opportunities. If you call yourself a leader, you need to lead, which includes continually sharpening your people skills. Rather than accepting the status quo perspective that "young people just don't get it," face the reality that a business without young people (Millennials, Gen Z…) has no future.

What Do You Do If You Are Being Yelled At?

For those entering the workforce, remember that you need to grow if you want to advance. Growth comes with experience. Experience is more often gained as you learn from mistakes than from success. Mistakes are part of the journey and they will be treated differently by each person in a position of leadership. Instruction and correction comes in many packages and one of those will be yelling. Believe me when I tell you, I know a thing or two about being yelled at. There is a big difference between:

Being yelled at for no good reason, for something you had nothing to do with, by someone with ill intent, and;

Being yelled at for something that makes sense, for something you played a significant role in, by someone with good intentions.

Again, we are talking about culture so I would like the record to show that yelling should not be the default nor the norm, but you must also understand that not all yelling is the same. People who care about their organization, culture and employees will have to provide training and correction. Yelling is not the same as instruction. If you are a manager and you are prone to outbursts at work, you are undermining your progress and you should look at the underlying causes.

If you are being yelled at by someone in a position of leadership, you should ask yourself if you did something that warranted being yelled at? Some of you may be of the mind that no one should ever be yelled at for any reason. For me, this has not been true as there have been moments where being yelled at has led to breakthroughs of clarity that otherwise would not have been achieved. One of those being the example I shared on that deck with my uncle where he exclaimed, "Why don't I have any screws in my hand?"

If you have never been yelled at it can be jarring. Some people have difficulty receiving any type of criticism, correction or discipline. If you did something wrong, my suggestion would be to *own it*. Listen for the truth in what is being said, regardless of how it is being said. If someone is losing their composure in the moment, the best thing you can do is to keep yours. After they have calmed down and you have had a chance to process the entirety of the interaction, you can decide if this is a place that you want to remain in and/or whether further action is necessary.

One of the healthiest things an organization can do is to teach their managers NOT to seek blame, but to teach their teams through mistakes, errors and failures. John Wooden, who dominated college basketball for 12 years including 7 national championships in a row with the UCLA Bruins, said, "A coach is someone who can give correction without causing resentment." If you are not familiar with coach Wooden I would encourage you to look him up. He was a master of having standards and drawing the best out of his players including some strong personalities like Kareem Abdul-Jabbar and Bill Walton.

As an organization, we want to set a precedence that keeping our emotions under control, even when we are upset for valid reasons, is the expectation. By removing blame, keeping your cool and having a process for dealing with errors, team members understand that when they mess up it will be something that they can own and conquer rather than being fearful that it will be a termination sentence for them.

When you are being disciplined at work, you may think, "I did something wrong but I don't deserve to be treated like this." You may be right. I learned early on that I can and should learn from everyone, even the jerks. As a career minded professional, you may find it helpful to ask yourself:

Intent

Is this person trying to help you (in their own way)?
Can you determine if there is some good intent even if you don't like the way the message is delivered?
What is the truth in what they are saying that you can use to better yourself?

Value

Does this person have something valuable that they can teach you?
Can you weather the storm for 3, 6, 9 or 12 months so that you can learn what you need to learn in order to set yourself up for the next opportunity?
What will you gain if you give the process some time?

Duration

Will this person dial back their intensity once you have proven yourself?
Do they view themselves as a drill sergeant in the military

and once you learn the necessary skills you will be treated differently?

Or, is it clear that regardless of what you do and why, they will always act this way?

Not All People in a Position of Leadership Were Trained to Lead

Typically, an employee who exhibits some skill or proficiency in aspects of their organization's production are promoted to a position of leadership. Many promotions come because someone has put their time in, earned their stripes or they were the only one dumb enough to take on the responsibilities. Just because they were promoted does not mean that they were chosen because they fit a clear skill set relevant to the role or received ample training on how to function in their position.

Most people in business are aware of the *Peter Principle*, whereby a person with potential is promoted to the point of incompetence. In his book *Traction*, Gino Wickman adds another perspective that is helpful for all parties when thinking about leadership roles, GWC. Building upon the concept of having the right people in the right seats from Jim Collins book *Good To Great*, Wickman states that the right candidate to own the responsibilities of promotion must:

G - Get It
W - Want It, and
C - Have the Capacity For It

Wickman states, "*A 'no' on any of these three mean it's not the right seat for the person, it's not their Unique Ability. You must not fool yourself on this point.*"[8]

If your organization is promoting people for reasons that are not in alignment with vision and values, you will struggle to clarify your culture as you are demonstrating that it does not drive your most important decisions. A business that has words on the wall but does not put the effort in to live by them is actively producing a lack of clarity.

If your organization is not training managers and holding them accountable to the culture, nothing else will matter in the way of building a culture until you fix these deficiencies. Our friends at *Arcade Wayfinding* call this "Promotion without Preparation,"[9] and beyond undermining your progress, it is also a factor in psychological safety for employees.

As a career minded professional, you will have to decide whether yelling, or anything else that you perceive to be negative, is enough to stall you from pursuing your vision with the team you are on. Will the grass be greener if you choose to go somewhere else or is there something to be gained by staying with this team and learning from this leader? Managers should not make assumptions about their team members nor should employees make assumptions about their managers. Good things happen when we treat people the way we would want to be treated - which often starts with treating each other as individuals.

If you are an employee working to climb the ladder, be F-A-T. If your manager doesn't have any screws in their hand, they might yell. If you don't want them to yell, put some screws in their hand.

If you want your team members to buy-in to the vision and live your organizational values, you must communicate the story of how these values came to be, how they translate to advancement for employees, and do so in a manner that they can be executed consistently.

You wouldn't buy-in to a business as an entrepreneur unless you could see the potential for real value as a return for your investment. Team members are making those same decisions, whether or not there is a good enough opportunity with your organization to invest their time in helping you build on your vision. The most effective people in a position of leadership find means to translate a vision worth buying-in to rather than lamenting why no one will buy-in. Compelling managers inspire more than they require.

Recruit, Onboard, and Train with Culture

My onboarding speech to most employees was very similar; those who have worked with me in management could probably tell you what I am about to say. I usually told people a bit about my story, how if I could do it - anyone can. I would follow that up with my base expectations,

> "We are committed to your success as a member of our team and we will teach you how to be successful. What we need from you is to be honest, hard working and willing to learn [very similar to F-A-T]. I cannot make you honest, hardworking or willing to learn but if you will commit to those three things you will have a good opportunity to succeed."

I would usually ask them what those things meant to them so that we could understand where they were coming from. To set them up for success, I would explain that by **honest** I mean:

> "First, I don't like surprises. If you make a mistake, please make me aware right away. If you tell me something went wrong we can resource a solution together. For example if you break something make me aware immediately. If I hear about it from an angry customer we have far fewer options. Second, don't lie. Don't make stuff up to cover for yourself; just be honest. I can't guarantee that there won't be consequences but I can guarantee they will be worse if you lie."

Whatever you say, you must back it up with how you act. If how you act as a person in a position of leadership is different than what you say, change what you say, otherwise you aren't being honest as a manager and you cannot expect your team to do something that you don't do.

Hard working should be self explanatory but you must NEVER assume that people know what you mean. Often when you hire someone with experience you tend to think that you don't have to train them on the basics. In my experience this is the opposite, hiring someone trained by others usually means you have to work harder to break bad habits. I enjoy working with people who are honest, hardworking, willing to learn and don't have bad (or contradictory) habits from competitors.

For new employees or part time helpers, I would explain, "When in doubt, clean." One key to not feeding the perception that you don't have value to the team is to always have a broom in your hand. If there is standby time, check with your supervisor whether there is something productive that needs to be done. If there isn't anything specific to do or you are awaiting instruction, grab a broom and start sweeping, grab a rag and start wiping things down, wash a vehicle, empty the trash. Standing around with nothing to do is one of the quickest ways to communicate that you have a little value.

There is a lot to learn and we are making a commitment to teach you. **Willing to Learn** means that you will listen, take the information in, ask questions as needed and will do your best to apply that information to your work. If you have a question you need to ask it, but as you go about your training process start to move from asking questions to confirming your own thoughts on what you think solutions are.

How you communicate and how you train are vital to realizing your culture. Communicating clearly at the point of hire is essential to set the expectations early and to follow that through with a consistent process for development.

The Training Process:

Phase 1

Management: We tell you, we show you, and we do it with you.

Employee: Starting out, you know little. You ask a lot of questions about how to do things and why we do them the way we do them. You do your best to act on the information you have been given. Most of what you do is under direct supervision.

Phase 2

Management: We continue to tell you and show you, but now you perform the work while we observe.

Employee: You know some things. Rather than asking basic questions of how to do things, you are asking questions to confirm if your thoughts on how to do them are correct. You are beginning to initiate work without assistance.

Phase 3

Management: You initiate the work and do the bulk of it without direct supervision. Supervisors confirm work has been completed to standard.

Employee: Most of your questions have to do with unique scopes of work that you haven't dealt with before, higher level execution or ideas on how something may be done better. You primarily work without direct supervision.

Phase 4

Management: The training process is designed to enable the team to clearly and consistently educate, demonstrate, and replicate team members who know how to Do it Right, Do it Efficiently, and Do it Excellently. As has been noted, efficiency and excellence cannot be achieved until the foundation of doing it right has been laid.

Employee: You have experience with most of the products and/or services that the organization offers. You are self-directed in your work and are beginning to help train new people through the same process that you went through.

For team members to buy-in there must be something clearly communicated that is worth buying-in to.

CHAPTER 3

*What is Culture and Why
Should I Care?*

Encouragement for Organizations

By Jon Isaacson

There have been plenty of lean years over the course of my career. Even when I started making some real money, we spent a lot of time digging out of holes from prior years. Even so, my beautiful wife has done an amazing job making even the simplest of holidays a thing of anticipation in our home. Whether it's red plastic flutes with sparkling cider for Valentine's Day or green pancakes on Saint Patrick's Day, our kids look forward to the small surprises.

I've tried in small ways to take this energy to teams that I have managed. I can remember a carpet cleaner who had been with the company nearly 15 years and he didn't even get a phone call from the regional manager. We mounted a carpet knife to a piece of wood, spray painted it gold, and sang him a song at our all staff meeting. It doesn't take much to let people know you see them and are genuinely grateful for their contribution.

One early morning I was in a grocery store picking up a two dollar birthday card and ten dollars in scratch-it's. The woman helping me asked if it was someone's birthday. I said it was and that I was just trying to do something fun, "Who knows, maybe they'll hit big!" She then shared with me that it was her 25th year anniversary. She asked, "Do you know what they got me?" With an awkward hopefulness in my voice, I said, "A really nice cake?" She told me that not only did they not get her a cake or even some crusty cookies, no one said anything and her manager threatened her job if she didn't come in and cover for someone who had called out.

We can do better. It doesn't take much to be a P-E-R-S-O-N in a position of leadership who treats P-E-O-P-L-E like people. While most of you reading this likely don't set out to do those things which you swore you would "never do" if you were "ever in charge," you have to be honest with where you are if you are going to make it better. We often make it more complicated than it is.

What Culture is and What Culture is Not.

Being intentional with your culture IS making an investment in your long term success.

Being intentional with your culture IS NOT a guarantee of success.

Being intentional with your culture IS aligning the vision and values with your operations.

Being intentional with your culture IS NOT a promise that all of your current team members will buy-in or that you will never have people issues.

The founding fathers of the United States worded it well, "Life, liberty, and the pursuit of happiness." As an individual, no one is promising or responsible for your happiness, you have to define and pursue it yourself.

As a person in a position of leadership, you may question (often) whether anything you are doing is having an effect. Is the juice worth the squeeze? Someone framed it well in the following discussion between two managers:

> Manager #1 is questioning whether all the extra effort they have been putting into their team is going to yield a harvest of better results in production and profitability. They ask Manager #2,

> *"What happens if we invest in our people and they just go elsewhere?"*

> Manager #2 also questions the same things but thankfully today they have a moment of clarity. In response to Manager #1's concern they Socratically respond,

> *"What happens if we don't invest in our people and they stay?"*

Everything worthwhile, every innovation, requires an element of risk. If you keep doing what you've always done, you will not achieve what you always have. The second law of thermodynamics, entropy, dictates that without new energy your organization will deteriorate, as all things do. Lex Sisney, author of *Organizational Physics*, states that the success formula is integration over entropy. In layman's terms, entropy is chaos. Integration is the gathering energy and using it to align capabilities with opportunities.

Being intentional with your culture is working towards this optimal operation by reducing dysfunction and getting the process working up to its potential. Mr. Sisney says, "If you can solve the underlying conditions that are causing entropy to increase in your business, you'll roll more energy to the bottom line and have a stronger, more resilient, and high-performing organization."[10]

If you want a better culture, the first step is to STOP doing those things that are undermining your development. This alone will help your growth. You accelerate this reduction of dysfunction by STARTING to identify and act upon those habits that enhance your culture. Applying both the stop and the start and you will soon be making noticeable advances towards your goals.

Size Doesn't Matter When Building a Culture

I am thankful that one of my earliest managers viewed her role as more than simply running a business. As the owner and operator, she used her restaurant as a place to help young people find their first job; as well as plenty of others whom she provided an opportunity to start over. Several of the conversations that we had in that tiny drive-thru delved into life lessons that rose above work and helped shape the framework of my development.

Woody's was a compact, single site business so there wasn't a need for an in-depth organizational chart. Everyone knew that Sharon was in charge. Even though it was small, we had a system and production had to run on schedule or we would fall behind. Tomatoes were cut a certain way using a guided knife, lettuce was chopped in a particular manner, bags of french fries, onion rings, and tater tots were weighed for value, and the world-famous fry sauce was mixed following a precise, handwritten recipe. When rush hour came, there was no time to catch up, so everything had to be ready in the small window leading up to those dinner time dashes.

> Woody's employees knew how to:
> Do It Right
> Do It Efficiently
> Do It Excellently

Sharon knew that her people were important and she developed a process that was clear so that our production was consistent. As we grew in confidence and demonstrated our ability to hold down the fort, she allowed us to run and close the drive-thru by ourselves. Sharon took chances with people that she believed in and leveraged responsibility to create a sense of ownership.

> Sharon's process had:
> Clarity
> Consistency
> Accountability

When new employees came on, we were proud of our process and our standards so we held people accountable; even as high schoolers working part time. I didn't know it yet, but this may have been where I first saw the power of clarity, consistency and accountability in action. My boss and friend, Sharon, showed me that even if something is small, with the right people and processes, you can build a sustainable business. You can create a sense of meaning and connection, even in a tiny drive-thru. Sharon has since passed but her daughter is still running the Woody's operation in Moses Lake, Washington with the same culture alive and well.

Additionally, Sharon understood that we were active and hungry high schoolers. We were allowed to make something to eat and were trusted to be responsible. As I will discuss in my upcoming chapter *Planted in the Middle*, food is a powerful tool in the quest for building and enhancing culture. Food can be an ice breaker for a meeting and a means of setting a more familiar atmosphere with a group.

One thing that has worked for me was having a fridge stocked with soda, water, refreshers, and energy drinks. We had a small jar where employees would pay a fraction of the cost to help keep the refreshments flowing. I often paid out of pocket to get the system started and apart from a few reminders (possibly some threats) the crews have honored the system. We eventually added trail mix, granola bars, soon discovering that Cup-O-Noodle was a big hit. While you don't want your team to linger when there is work to be done, there is a lot of value when they choose to hang out while doing their paperwork, during breaks, or at the end of a shift.

A business that cannot attract new talent will die. You need new employees in order to grow your team. You need to grow in your understanding of the current and incoming workforce to remain competitive, as in today's market your ability to hire and develop candidates is at least as important as your ability to find new clients. New people also means new eyes and fresh perspectives. So many good questions come from new people who ask, "Why do you do it that way?"

With intentionality, you can build a culture that will help you thrive. You don't have to yell, but you do need to be clear. You can teach young people and old, even high schoolers, to be F-A-T so that they can grasp and live out your vision and values. If you've ever had the pleasure of seeing your team members communicate with clarity, operate with consistency, and hold each other accountable, you have witnessed the beauty of the return on investment in culture.

The Culture Question

In business, the question with regards to culture is not whether your organization has a culture. The question you should be asking is whether your culture has evolved by chance or because you have been intentional in developing it.

If you are still questioning whether your organization has a culture, you may find it more productive to ask whether your organization has a shared mindset and habits.

Do you have a shared mindset for success?

Is your message (vision / values) clear?

Do you have shared habits that enhance your ability to achieve your goals?

Is your process consistent?

Are the vision and values lived by everyone in the organization, from top to bottom and bottom to top?

Is your team accountable to and for each other?

I have been a part of many teams. As I start my next venture, I shared with my partners that in my observation the dysfunction in many companies is not that any one person isn't working hard but rather they are not rowing in the same direction. If you have three partners, all eager to do well, and all rowing with 100% of their strength, you can all be working hard and yet going nowhere because you are rowing in circles.

In such a scenario the key thing that needs to change is not more effort, which will lead to only going faster on the carousel, but to take a short break from rowing so that you can get in alignment with the direction of your efforts. Applying your energy to developing your culture in this way is part of the process of getting everyone on the same page, rowing in the same direction, so that you can make progress in your process.

As you go from rowing in circles to splitting the waves in the same direction, that sense of collective achievement reduces entropy. You can see what Lex Sisney calls integration in action, whereby the team is *using energy efficiently to align capabilities with opportunities.*

In the status quo organization, the vision, the values, and the culture come from the top down. The big wigs get together and "brainstorm". Someone prints these lofty ideals up on something fancy and posts them on the walls, adds them to the website, and has the local managers hand them out to everyone in their offices on 3x5 cards.

And *voila* we have a thriving culture, right?

If you are reading this book, I trust that you know I am being sarcastic and you are also tired of trying things that don't work.

I have assembled a group of my friends to share their lessons learned from the trenches. You can shorten your DANG learning curve by applying these practical experiences to your efforts in relationship to culture.

I have heard many people mentioning that culture is a competitive advantage. What I hope to do in this book is to help you see that your efforts to develop your culture are:

Worthwhile

Within your realm of control

Less complicated than you think

Every entrepreneur seeks sustainable competitive advantages, we have written this book to help you make progress in yours. As a person in a position of leadership, regardless of what level of leadership you find yourself in, *you must control what you can control.*

This is a book by everyday people in positions of leadership, for everyday people in positions of leadership. As awesome as my friends are, this book will not solve all your problems, but hopefully you will understand that first, you are not alone in your quest and second, you have a network of people who are willing to help you achieve your goals.

In early 2019, I started a series of Youtube videos that would serve as the foundation for what would evolve into The DYOJO Podcast. It actually started as *Three Questions with a Pro* as a sub-segment of my monthly column *The Intentional Restorer* for Restoration and Remediation Magazine (R&R).

My goal with the podcast is to help those in the skilled trades to shorten their DANG learning curve for personal and professional development. Anyone who has achieved any level of success is at that level, not because they are smarter than you but, because they have learned the lessons they needed to learn and applied the information correctly. Learning from others helps you to accelerate your own momentum and should help you avoid making the same mistakes.

As you dig into the examples shared by my talented troupe of co-authors, the core question is - *what are some of the small things that have helped to enhance or undermine culture* in their experiences? The idea being that small steps in the right direction will help you build your vision more expediently. A strong culture, like a good rudder or skilled cockswain, will help you all to row in the same direction.

Input vs. Output

If you think in terms of inputs and outputs, in positions of leadership your strategic thinking relates to your vision and goals for growing externally and your cultural efforts relate to how you develop from within. In order to achieve your goals you need to be in alignment with your vision from within. The ideas cannot flow as edicts from the upper crust down to the bottom dwellers and somehow produce sustainable results. You must find ways to identify and develop your values from the ground up.

As we discussed on their podcast *Blue Collar Nation*, my friends Eric Sprague and Larry Wilberton encourage business owners that you have to market your message internally to your team as consistently and passionately as you do externally to your clients. This dynamic duo sold a successful property restoration company that they built from scratch. Many of the key lessons that they learned they now share as daily soft skills training for technicians in service based businesses through their new company *Morning Tech Meeting*.

You must communicate, train, and hold your team members accountable for the cultural values (inputs) if you want those cultural distinctives to translate through your services to your clients (outputs). Those in a position of leadership who can learn to communicate effectively with their team members and inspire them to live the vision will see more consistent and sustainable results in their businesses.

In short, culture is what you are as an organization. Your culture is the culmination of your mindset and habits. Culture is what you [all] do. You cannot make up a culture, but you certainly can foster the mindset and develop the habits that will help your team to embrace and enhance the vision.

In addition to being an author, Lex Sisney, whom I mentioned at the opening of this chapter, is a business scaling expert. He was generous enough with his time to join me for The DYOJO Podcast to discuss *Growing Your Business Without Compromising Your Values*[11]. He offers a framework for what he calls *The Culture System* on his website in which he says,

> "You can't dictate culture. But you can design for it. A strong culture system is designed around four key elements: Values, Rituals, Stories, and Consequences."[12]

If your goal is to have a healthy and thriving team, culture is the means through which you care for your organization. If you can identify, build, and staff around a culture that enhances your values, then your combined efforts will have greater focus and potency. The development of a culture becomes, through the process, a means of attracting, fostering, and retaining good team members. In short, take care of the culture because the culture is what cares for your people.

If you care for your people, your team members will be enabled and energized to care for your customers. In service based companies, your people on the ground and in the field are the ones who have the bulk of the hands-on interaction with your customers.

Team members that are cared for will care about the team and will do work that communicates care on through to your clientele.

Your culture is unique and your people are unique so the culture is always evolving as you all develop. The end goal is the same, create positive customer experiences so that your combined efforts create value that people will gladly pay for as you continue to build your business.

All companies need revenue in order to function, but we often forget that at the end of the line those dollars come from people (your customers). We want our customers to appreciate the value that we bring to them. Customers that care about your products and/or services are won over by people that care (about your vision and values) and have been cared for (by your culture). Therefore being intentional about caring is one of the most profitable aspects of your business that you can focus your efforts on.

If you seek to control what you can control, be intentional with your culture. A strong culture, one that cares for your team members, is not a unicorn (jargon) it is a gold mine (differentiator).

The Benefits of Culture

We know bad culture when we see it, yet it may not always lend itself to clear definitions. If you are still reading this book than you understand that:

Taking care of your culture is critical to taking care of your people.

Taking care of your people is essential to taking care of your customers.

Taking care of your customers is the foundation of a sustainable business.

Therefore, developing, adapting, and caring for your culture is vital to your vitality as an organization. Your **input** of time, effort, and resources towards developing an intentional culture is directly linked to achieving optimal business **outputs**.

Every business wants, and needs, to be profitable. Yet, you do not make profits appear from thin air. You must have a product and/or service. You need to hire people to assist you in providing those products and/or services if you want to scale your business. As you grow you need to create systems as you develop a culture that seeds, feeds, weeds, and harvests for profitability.

Profitability is an effect, not a cause.

In the same way, you cannot snap your fingers to make a good culture appear. You must define, develop, and defend your cultural process. As you do so, culture plays a role in attracting, hiring, training, disciplining, promoting, and progressing within your organization.

Your culture is enhanced or undermined by what you don't do as much as by what you do. Mr. Sisney articulated the role of rituals and consequences. Former Navy Seal Jocko Wilinik adds to these concepts when he states, "No matter what has been said or written, if substandard performance is accepted and no one is held accountable—if there are no consequences—that poor performance becomes the new standard."[13]

Your team members are watching you to see if the cultural rituals and consequences are empty concepts, whether they are for everyone or if you are just another status quo organization that applies them selectively.

If you are in a position of leadership, you have to remember all of those items you said you would do differently if you ever got the chance. Today is that day; the time is now. Culture consists of the mindset and habits that flow from within your organization. Your organization is made up of people who are either:

Group 1: Attempting to do business in alignment with your culture. ENGAGED

Group 2: Going about their business the best they know how, regardless of your culture.

Group 3: Actively working against your culture.

Group 3 should be self explanatory, but you learn a lot from meeting with your detractors and asking them why they aren't on the same page with you. There may be a few in the group who have some valid insights and may even be able to be brought back from the dark side.

Unfortunately, those in Group 1 and 2 may be trying to be "on the same page" with your vision and values but may be unclear about what the objectives are. They may be giving 100% effort as they row, but like the partners I mentioned, if they aren't rowing in the same direction they will be working hard only to spin in circles. As a manager, you may think employees are working against you when the underlying problem is they don't know what rowing with the crew looks like because you and/or the organization have not made it clear.

Where do we start?

Clarity. Clarify the vision.

Consistency. Build consistency in the values.

Accountability. Develop a process that holds everyone (from top to bottom) accountable to making progress.

The mindset and habits of your people impact how your organization does business. Your people are your culture. Are you ready for a long run-on sentence? If you want to direct your culture with intentional inputs, with the hopes that doing so will lead to clearer and more consistent outcomes (output), as a person in a position of leadership you have to constantly find ways to address the mindset and habits at all levels of the team.

As we continue to dig into this subject matter, the question we are asking is: What are some of the *small things* that have helped to *enhance* or *undermine* culture in the experiences of our talented group of authors?

PART 1:

*How Small Things Enhance
Your Culture*

CHAPTER 4

Don't Call Me Manager

By Luke Draeger

When I was young, I wanted to be a firefighter. It's a common aspiration for children, along with other glory seeking vocations—police officer, physician, actor, professional athlete. Never once did I––or any other child in history for that matter––utter the words, "When I grow up, I'd love to be a manager."

You don't witness kids play-acting the role of a prototypical middle manager. Imagine it: Little Billy dressed in a polo and khakis, oversized key ring hanging from his belt, pacing the room in frustration, wringing hands over the fact that his imaginary auto parts store is behind goal pace for the month; meanwhile he's rehearsing his forced smile for the regional vice-president, who will be visiting from corporate later this week. It's not the sort of job a young person dreams about, but many of us, despite all plans to the contrary, wind up as managers at some point.

My entire working life, companies have wanted to put me in charge of things. It's rarely been something I've sought after; in fact, I've often retreated from the opportunity to advance into management. It's difficult enough for me to manage myself, much less be responsible for the performance of others. Yet, over and over, I've been moved into leadership roles. I've been told by some that it's because of my voice. I have a deep baritone, and I like to talk a lot, so people often listen to me, regardless of whether or not I have anything smart to say.

My first official leadership role came at a restaurant where I worked the front counter. The owner discovered I was pretty good at explaining how to take food orders and operate the cash register, so he put me in a position to train new hires. Being just fifteen years of age, the situation was a bit awkward for me. Despite the fact that every person I trained was significantly older than me, I came to enjoy it. My enjoyment ended the day I was asked to train a young woman who was completely incapable of counting change correctly. The frustrating two hour training session culminated in the woman quitting in a fit of tears before her first shift ended.

I didn't escape my teen years before finding myself in additional supervisory roles. While still in high school, I became assistant manager of a *Mrs. Field's* cookie store, where I again found myself managing employees several years older than I was. One employee, a spirited young man in his twenties with an appetite for partying, correctly presumed that I was more interested in being his buddy than his manager. He took advantage by indulging in excessively long breaks and occasionally guzzling beer in the back room. This was my first lesson in the immutable fact that managerial jobs are often granted, not to those best equipped to manage, but instead go to those who demonstrate a propensity to work hard and show up on time. In the years following I would learn that this same problem—that of placing employees in roles for which they're ill-suited—is one that plagues the majority of organizations and is the root of much dysfunction in the modern workplace. More on that later.

By the time I reached my late twenties, I'd had stints as a supervisor for a janitorial firm, team leader for a youth program with the YMCA, head tutor for a college writing center, and night manager of a valet parking facility. It was during a particularly frustrating shift at the valet lot, following a personal blow up inspired by one of my undependable employees ghosting his shift, that I determined I was finished trying to manage people. At least, I thought I was.

Through the recommendation of a friend, I found myself working as a project manager for a small water damage restoration firm. Though my position was still managerial in nature, my job was only to manage the dry out projects; very rarely did I have to manage people. This was welcome relief after a decade and half of what I considered to be a long series of babysitting gigs. As it turns out, my years in emergency service work are the closest I've ever come to my childhood dream of becoming a firefighter. I wasn't saving lives, of course, but saving people's property seemed close enough.

It's been said that Fate is not without a sense of humor. Fate must have been laughing hysterically when, after nearly a decade in the turbulent field of emergency services, I accepted the position of store manager for the Seattle branch of one of the largest specialty cleaning and restoration suppliers in the country. By this time, I'd had over eight years of industry experience under my belt. I brought some much coveted tribal knowledge to the job, but it wasn't my industry experience that made me most attractive to my new employer; it was my management experience. The store I took over was the organization's newest and was suffering all the inevitable problems and challenges that come with a new location. It was my job to fix it.

The staff was small—a counter person, outside sales rep, and two service technicians. The location was under-performing, and the assumption was that the staff was to blame for the lousy numbers. Not wanting to create too much turmoil at the start of my tenure, I determined that for the first six months I would work with the hand I was dealt and try to avoid making any staffing changes. A rapid turnover of employees often signifies instability, which can lead to a bad experience for customers.

It was during these early months that I received a wise bit of advice from one of my customers, advice that has stuck with me through the years since. This man (I'll call him Scott) was the owner of a small restoration firm, a recent venture for him. In the decades prior, he'd made a career as a corporate trouble-shooter. Companies would hire him to come in, analyze their systems and procedures, and recommend necessary changes. Scott loved to talk as much as I did; whenever he visited the store, I knew I was in for some fascinating conversation. One day, Scott was describing the steps he was taking to handle the growth his new company was experiencing, and he said those sticky words I've never forgotten: "When you take a good employee and put them in a lousy system, the system is going to win every time."

I pondered those words for a long time. How did this idea apply to my situation as a manager tasked with raising a sinking ship? Did every sailor on this ship need to be replaced, or was a lousy system to blame? The answer turned out to be a little of both. A couple of my employees were consistently poor performers—often late to work, constantly distracted, low producers—but others showed signs they were capable of helping get the store on track, given proper encouragement.

My front counter person (I'll call her Diane), was one of the promising ones. Diane was consistent, punctual, and put forth a solid effort every day. Even better, the customers liked her. Her chief short-coming was that she seemed completely incapable of *selling*—a crucial weakness for an individual serving as the first point of sale contact in the store. At first, I thought the problem was lack of product knowledge. To help with this, I initiated training sessions. Each week, I would assign a product to each employee, give them a few days to research, and have them present what they'd learned about the product during the next meeting. It didn't take long for me to realize that Diane had plenty of knowledge about our products, more than enough to effectively help customers with their purchases. Her challenge was with communication.

I learned this during one training session in which I asked the employees to role play. I played the role of the customer asking for help; the employees were to play the salespeople. Almost all salespeople, even experienced ones, dislike role playing. There's something extremely awkward about playing a game of pretend in front of your colleagues. It's sort of like having an out loud conversation with yourself and then finding out someone was listening in on you the whole time. Diane loathed role playing, so much so that she cried when I asked her to do it. She wasn't just being dramatic; she actually suffered emotional distress, akin to paralyzing stage fright. When I spoke with her about it, she said she just wasn't confident she knew what she was talking about. But I knew that wasn't her problem. The knowledge was there; she just couldn't find a way to get it out.

After months of prodding her to elevate her sales performance, I resigned myself to the idea that Diane would never improve. I'd either have to stumble along with a weak salesperson at the front counter, or I'd need to replace her with someone better.

Then a miracle happened—not a grandiose *parting of the Red Sea* type of miracle, but the small, every day sort we tend to take for granted. A child's first words might be a proper comparison, only Diane wasn't the one who needed to learn to speak better; I was. I needed to learn to speak Diane's language. It happened by lucky coincidence, thanks to a new program the company rolled out.

A year or so into my tenure, the company started an upselling program for all front counter people. Each month, the brand managers would choose one product they wanted to highlight. Every store received increased stock of that month's featured item, and the counter people were encouraged to ask every customer if they'd like to add this particular item to their order. (The cleaning supply store equivalent to the pervasive question of many fast food workers: *You want fries with that?*) As an incentive, the counter persons were rewarded with spiffs for every sale of the featured item. The bonuses were small, usually a dollar or two, but they added up, boosting some of the more successful employees' checks by hundreds of dollars. There were weekly emails from the national sales manager as well, ranking the performances of the various counter people, lauding those who were moving the most product. Knowing Diane's shortcomings where it came to selling, I didn't expect much from her. She surprised me.

The first couple months were tentative. Diane made a small difference in sales by simply asking every customer if they wanted to add the item of the month to their order. No frills, no explanation of why the customer might find the item useful, just a quick *"You want one of these?"* Some customers said yes because they really could use the item, some said yes because Diane was a friendly person, and they wanted to help her out. The impact was nominal. The weekly reports ranking the various counter persons' success found Diane near the bottom of the list. This began to change a few months later.

I walked by the front counter one day to find Diane squinting at her computer screen. I asked her what she was doing, and she told me she was designing a sign for the following month's featured item. She'd noticed the small increase to her paycheck the previous couple months, and she wanted to make those increases a bit more substantial. Turned out, the sales spiff was an effective motivator, though I would find out later it wasn't money that ultimately took Diane to the next level. The sign she came up with wasn't fancy, just a brief description of the item, a heavy duty carpet cleaning chemical our company manufactured, along with a graphic of an orange being squeezed––appropriate for the product, since it contained a citrus additive. The sign eventually became the centerpiece of a display she built with chemical boxes, along with another sign indicating customers could receive a discount if they purchased a full case. Diane's sales increased a bit more that month, along with her motivation to do even more the month following.

Over the course of that year, I watched Diane's product displays become more and more creative. It began to occur to me that I'd had her all wrong. Diane really could sell. The problem was never her; it was me. I'd assumed that because she struggled to communicate verbally, she couldn't do it at all. But Diane was finding a different way to communicate.

Every day, Diane spent her lunch break drawing what she called "a doodle." She created these eye-bending spiral designs on little square pieces of drawing paper. I think it was therapeutic for her, making those doodles. Having watched her create so many drawings, I should have realized sooner that Diane was an artist, a *visual* communicator. Through her product displays, she managed to parlay her natural creative talents into a way to excel at her job.

With better and more elaborate displays came better sales. I began sending pictures of Diane's work to the national sales manager, and the images made their way into the company newsletter. Other counter people in other locations took Diane's lead and started creating their own amazing displays. Eventually, awards were given for the month's best display. Most months, Diane won the award. Her most memorable display was during the month of November. The highlighted product was our proprietary carpet protector chemical. Diane set up a table to look like a classic Thanksgiving feast. Seated atop the table was a cartoonish looking turkey statue, made to look like it had been drinking wine and managed to spill it all over the carpet below. The fake wine was pooled up on the protected carpet, demonstrating that even a messy party animal like Tom Turkey was no match for our incredible carpet protector.

This experience demonstrated to me that the biggest error a manager can make is to treat an employee like a machine—as if you can simply place the employee where you need her, press the correct sequence of buttons, and *Presto!*, job handled, box checked. You see this mistake all the time—employees put into positions or situations for which they are poorly suited. I could never have trained Diane into becoming comfortable speaking about products. There was something fundamental inside her which prevented her from being able to do this. I might as well have been asking a five foot tall person to stock the upper shelves without a set of stairs.

I made a similar mistake more than once when hiring people for my service department. The store was always short on mechanics, so any time I interviewed an individual who claimed even a modicum of technical skill, I would hire him on the spot, only to discover the hard way this person was *not* a mechanic. Our company invested heavily in training programs for our service people; they would fly employees out of state to participate in manufacturer training and send them to other branch locations to be mentored by more seasoned service people. I wince when I think of the resources we wasted trying to train up people who had little chance of success as small equipment mechanics.

I don't care much for the term "train up". It suggests that the only obstacle blocking a person's success is lack of knowledge. Give the person knowledge, *train her up*, and the sky's the limit. I believe we do ourselves and our employees a better service when we stop trying to train up and learn to train forward. By train forward, I mean we take time to identify an employee's natural talents and find ways to help them utilize those skills in a way that benefits both the individual and the company.

It starts with paying attention. Who is this person? What sorts of things does she naturally excel at? What types of activities energize her and provoke her to want to do well? Once you're able to answer these types of questions, it becomes easier to determine whether or not an employee is right for a particular position. You may find someone who was mediocre in one department becomes a star in another. Or you may have someone like Diane—a competent customer service person who just needed to be granted the freedom to sell in a way that played to her strength as a creative. Once I understood this about her, I was able to train her *forward* by suggesting ways she could share product information visually, rather than verbally.

An interesting side effect to Diane's growing success began to occur. Our struggling little Seattle branch, once an object of pity among the staff of other locations, now had something to be proud of. We were finally good at something. I don't think it's a coincidence that the basis for our pride had roots in creativity. We tend to put people in categories of creative and non-creative, but I think that's a fallacy.

It's true, some folks are more skilled at making things than others, but it seems to me that everybody enjoys the practice of creating. Take the most left-brained, linear thinker who's barely capable of drawing a recognizable stick figure, put him at a table with a group of kids decorating gingerbread figures, and watch that "non-creative" person turn his little cookie into a sugary art piece. Even if the thing turns out ugly, he'll still take pride in it. He'll compare it to the work of his fellow decorators and may even snap pictures to post on social media. It's a universal attribute of humans: we like to make things, and we tend to like the things we've made.

Over the months, I observed Diane's creative energy catch on with others—the service guys in particular. Anybody who's ever managed a service department knows all too well that one of the hardest challenges is maintaining a clean, organized work area. (I understand there must be clean mechanics in the world, but I've never met one.) Despite my best efforts to coerce my mechanics into keeping things clean, the service area was a perpetual pigsty. After a year of frustration, I finally thought to engage the service people's creativity.

I sat down with my two service workers and asked them if they agreed the service center needed to be kept much cleaner than it had been. They agreed, and I invited them to come up with their own solution to the problem. They created a chart, which broke down the service area into eight different stations. Each of them took responsibility for half of the stations and agreed they would make sure their assigned area was kept clean and organized. The improvement came quickly, and it was significant. The difference was that I let them come up with their own solution to a problem rather than force my own ideas upon them. I encouraged them to engage their creativity, which made the job feel less like work and more like fun.

The story of my tenure as manager of that supply store ended with a Store of the Year award. The accolade didn't prevent me from stepping away from the position after six years. I experienced plenty of success there, but too many years of acting as the proverbial fish out of water took a toll on me. You'll recall, I began this chapter describing my reluctance over the years to accept management positions. It's a reluctance that remains to this day. I'm in sales now, once again responsible only for myself. Still, offers of managerial jobs come along with comical frequency. If history is any indication, I'll likely find myself in that role again one day. I suppose if I ever do accept another management position, I'll insist I not be cursed with the title of manager. It's just not who I am. Call me a teacher if you want, or an observer and exploiter of people's natural abilities. On my best day, you may even call me an inspirer. Just don't call me a manager.

CHAPTER 5

Say Thank You

By Lisa Lavender

Gratitude is powerful; it can feed a culture of excellence, exceptional service to others, pride, and happiness.

When I go to a restaurant and the drink I ordered is placed in front of me, I say "Thank you" with a smile. The person serving me may perceive me as "nice." It may be, for a split second, that I made them feel appreciated. The server continues to provide excellent service because I am grateful and made them feel respected.

"Thank you" is representative of a wide variety of small gestures that communicate appreciation. In our day-to-day it may take many forms:

Thumbs up

Pat on the back

A smile with an enthusiastic, "WOW!"

A text with an emoji, "TY."

Saying, "thank you" is natural for some, but not all. Even those who naturally express gratitude, at times, may forget to show appreciation for those they rely on and appreciate the most. Anyone at any time, may find themselves going out of their way to thank a stranger for something incidental while neglecting those we care about and appreciate the most. In a company culture that is void of appreciation, people may become unmotivated and feel devalued. Resentment and lack of engagement can take over and become counterproductive to the culture you are trying to build or maintain.

Appreciation is a word that can make some budget conscious leaders cringe; often appreciation is followed by something that involves money, a line item in the budget. "Thank you" requires minimal resources. You can supercharge your culture with small gestures of appreciation.

"Thank You" The Superfuel

Regardless of your position, placement in a reporting line, or industry, you have a stake in your company culture. Everyone in an organization can impact and influence culture. Small gestures of appreciation will benefit individuals in their careers, positively impact colleagues, and ultimately contribute to the success of the organization and its operations.

As we consider the power of everyone in the organization impacting our culture in our organization, I bring your attention to In Speed of Trust by Stephen R. Covey.

Covey makes the case for the value of trust in business, leaders, and organizations. As Covey breaks down the elements that contribute to the abstract notion of trust, the first two levels are:

> Character: Integrity + Intent
>
> Competency: Capabilities + Results

As small gestures of appreciation and gratitude provide the superfuel to each other and the organization, it is only in the context that the foundation of the relationships and culture are built on trust. If a gesture of appreciation is not sincere or received with skepticism of someone's intent, it will not have the positive impact that is desired.

A Simple Gesture of Taking Someone to Lunch

A supervisor takes the team to lunch as a gesture of appreciation for completing a big project on time and budget.

With Trust: The team has a great lunch and celebrates the success of the team and the individuals. There is pride and everyone reflects on each other's positive contribution to the project. The team reciprocates the appreciation to the supervisor who is respected and trusted by the team. There is no doubt that the supervisor takes joy and pride in the team and is driven to be a positive impact on their success.

Voids of Trust: The supervisor has questionable intent and integrity in his gesture of lunch. The team goes to lunch because they have to go; they do not feel gratitude nor do they celebrate the achievement of the project. The supervisor's behaviors have made them lack trust in his intentions and integrity making the gesture meaningless to them. The supervisor seems to only care about his own numbers and he took them to lunch so that he would "look good" to others.

In *212 Degrees of Service*, author Mac Anderson shares "The 10 Rules of Creating a Service Culture." Mr. Anderson discusses the concept that "attitudes are contagious." This resonates as I walk into work, wheels spinning, stressed out, having driven in with my knuckles clenched around the steering wheel, and then being greeted by a co-worker wearing a big smile who enthusiastically says, "Good Morning! Have a Great Day!" My stress dissipates as I am compelled to smile and reply, "Thank you! You too!" Talk about a really small gesture; a simple sincere wish for my day to be "good." I am thankful for the sentiment. When we foster a culture that has and expresses gratitude, it simply becomes contagious at all levels of the organization.

A Simple Gesture of Opening the Door for Someone

Thank You: I often walk into work, hands overflowing with computers, lunch, and bags of "essentials" of the day. A co-worker scurries across the parking lot to simply open the door for me. They did this because they care and genuinely want to help me. I am thankful and express myself accordingly. I would have had to plop everything on the ground and dig through the bags for my key. It took very little energy and was actually quite natural. One particular day, my thank you for opening the door was returned by my co-worker thanking me for approving a new tool that was purchased for his team. It was a tool that contributed to their success and helped them improve their quality and efficiency when installing drywall. The expression of gratitude then made me feel good, happy, and the appreciation fuels me to provide more tools that help the team.

No Thank You: On the contrary, if someone were to open the door for their supervisor, and there was no eye contact, interaction, or acknowledgement of the gesture, the supervisor ignored the person and went to their office, what are we spreading? The contagion in this case, at the start of the day, is a cold and uncaring welcome, a lack of gratitude of a gesture to help; it could spread. Not only does it spread amongst the team, one of the points made in *212 Degrees of Service*, is that it will spread to customers and those served by the person, *"Because your people will only treat the customers as well as they are being treated."*

The Cases for "Thank You"

I often do a variety of nice things for the people that I work with and some say, "Thank you" and some do not acknowledge with any sign or gesture of appreciation. My motivation is never for any kind of praise or acknowledgement. However, I started to notice a slight twinge of annoyance inside towards the people who never say, "Thank you". I began to wonder, "Did anyone teach them to say, thank you?"

Then a song that played over and over in my home, 20 years ago, when my children were small, started ringing in my ears. Trust me, it is not a song you want stuck in your head, but there it was: *Say Please and Thank You* by Barney the Purple Dinosaur.

There are lots of things that we can do to be nice

Sometimes they are hard to remember...

But there are two little things, you should never forget

From January through December

We're talking about Please and Thank You

They're called the magic words

If you want nice things to happen, they're the words that should be heard

I considered making everyone listen to the song but that may be considered cruel. If you do play the song, a word of caution, it literally may get stuck in your head.

Why is the lack of "thank you," this small gesture of appreciation, so "annoying?" How can it be so detrimental to the company's culture? If something is not appreciated, one could say it is taken for granted or expected. One who has not been shown gratitude may feel unappreciated, have resentment, and may make assumptions about those who do not express any sign of appreciation. The reality is that many times the appreciation may exist but is simply not expressed or shown.

I run service organizations, all within the same industry, but with different customer types, business partners and services. The cases:

Case 1 – Students say Thank You

In our training services organization, it is part of our basic operating principles to be hospitable and deliver on our promise to provide "Knowledge, Passion, and Inspiration" for the success of students and their companies. Comfortable chairs, clean bathrooms, delicious food, and high-quality education are some of the fundamentals. The team is given on-going and unsolicited gratitude from the students. Little gestures, comments, and emails with, "Thank you so much." Sometimes the gratitude is directed towards a little detail that they particularly appreciated.

Impact to Culture: The gratitude fuels an intense drive and focus to not only maintain the process, procedures, and environment; but to keep improving it and making it better so that every time a student has an experience with us, we exceed their expectation. The individuals of the organization feel a sense of reward, fulfillment, and purpose from the gratitude of successfully impacting the lives of others through training.

Case 2 – Customer says Thank You

In my disaster restoration company, after a job is complete, the customer gets a survey and has a spot to write comments. These surveys are circulated to the team so that they can take a moment to celebrate their successes and get super charged by gratitude from customers. A little thank you with a big impact!

Impact to Culture: It refuels and energizes a team that at times works long hours, in difficult and challenging conditions. Sharing these small notes of gratitude from our customers with the team creates a sense of pride and achievement in successfully serving others during their most difficult times. As a small business owner, I love seeing how this promotes teamwork and elevates the role of successfully serving our clients.

Case 3 – Individuals say Thank You

A business partner is in a bind and asks you to get a report done by the end of the day. You go out of your way, juggle your schedule, and make it happen. After you submit the report, it feels great to get a nice reply of, "Thank you, I really appreciate your help."

Impact: If the person asks you for a favor in the future, you will likely be compelled to go out of your way again. The same applies when you ask a business partner to help you out; when they do, say "thank you."

Alternative: If you go out of your way to accommodate some-one, or ask someone to go out of their way to help you, the void of any sign of gratitude may have an unintended consequence of not getting the help needed next time.

As an individual when you express gratitude to those you work with not only are you positively impacting culture, but you are also helping with your own professional growth. If your boss takes you to lunch, say "thank you." You do not want to be per-ceived as ungrateful or entitled. If your direct report does some-thing well and on time that you requested, say "thank you, well done."

Impact: You are perceived as nice and approachable which leads to many important soft skills as one advances in their career, like the ability to collaborate, innovate, and problem solve with co-workers. Individuals who exemplify positive values in an organization often shine like stars.

Fostering "Thank You"

Small gestures of appreciation that have a big impact on your culture.

If the impact demonstrated in the cases above are so, let's get more of it going within your company. Nurturing and fostering gratitude within the company culture will have a positive im-pact. A void of this value can lead to a culture that wreaks with resentment, entitlement, and people who feel undervalued, un-appreciated and may not have a sense of purpose in contribut-ing to the mission and objectives of the organization.

Also, from an internal and external standpoint, you can get more things done and have more good things happen, when you are nice and say, "thank you." *Remember please and thank you, they are the magic words, if you want nice things to happen, they are the words that should be heard.*

Leadership: As with most things, it starts at the top. Leaders should show appreciation and set the example for others and it needs to be genuine.

Value statement: I believe that values that are important to a company along with the culture should be known and articulated. This allows you to clearly communicate the expectation when hiring and developing people. It also allows you to hold people accountable when they act contrary to the values. A value statement may look something like:

We appreciate and respect the time, talent, and contribution of every member of our team.

We value our external business relationships and appreciate their contribution to our organization's success.

Create buy in and make the case for outward expressions of appreciation:

There may be people who do not feel that you should have to thank someone for something that you are paying for whether it's a team member or a business partner.

There may also be people who are appreciative and grateful but do not either know how to express or as a matter of personality, simply do not.

Create mechanisms, programs, and initiatives that help everyone remember to thank each other. The world within your organization is moving fast and there are always challenges to tackle and things to get done. It is very easy to overlook or forget to express gratitude. It feels good to be thanked and propels us to want to do more; it feels good to express gratitude. A couple of ideas that I have implemented within my organization:

You Are Awesome Raffle:

It is a simple two-part form. At the top it says, YOU ARE AWESOME. Every person in the company is constantly encouraged to remember to thank a person with the, YOU ARE AWESOME ticket. I get them, put a smiley face on it and my initials. The nominated team member gets a copy and the other copy goes in a jar for a quarterly raffle. The point is everyone wins. I even get great joy at seeing the great, sometimes little and sometimes big, things that people are doing for each other and our customers. In addition, the expressions of gratitude amongst the team gives me the opportunity to say, "thank you" with the smiley face as I look at every ticket.

I caught someone...Company Meeting

At the end of every company meeting, we do an open mic where anyone can stand up, and share something specific that some-one else in the company did that was great or that they appreci-ated. It was initially an exercise to avoid focusing on problems and forgetting to celebrate all the things that are going right but it really turned into expressions of everyone's gratitude to each other. Ultimately, this platform helps everyone remember to say, "Thank you," and energizes the room while all feel joy and pride in the air. It encourages more of the great stuff to continue happening and inspires others as they hear the good things that others are doing that are gratitude worthy. It takes only a few minutes and becomes a machine of inspiration that fuels our team towards excellence.

I thank you, the reader, for choosing to read this. I am thankful because it simply brings me joy to have the opportunity to share my thoughts, experiences, and ideas that I have collected throughout my career. I sincerely hope that there may be a tid-bit that inspires you and helps your organization. May the culti-vation of this one *little thing* bring you continued success.

CHAPTER 6

Planted in the Middle

By Jon Isaacson

"**I** want it said of me by those who knew me best, that I always plucked a thistle and planted a flower where I thought a flower would grow." - Abraham Lincoln

Our goal in this chapter is in line with the goal of this book, to discuss how small things can enhance or undermine your effort to develop a strong culture. This is important because a solid culture is essential for remaining competitive in the current marketplace and will continue to grow in prominence as the speed of change accelerates in the coming years. Even as we evolve with innovation, the significance of developing our soft skills in leadership will be premium as attracting and keeping good talent will be the key to survival.

To clarify a few things, first let's define culture. You are your culture. Culture is a reflection of who you are and what you do as a team. The question is not whether you have a culture but how intentional you have been to develop the right culture. When you decide to transform your mindset from being *stuck* in the middle, to seeing yourself as having been *planted*, you empower yourself to make a positive impact.

Allow me to share my first example of how a small thing can

help shape the environment while also demonstrating how culture flows out of who you are and what you do.

Just a Mouthful of Donuts Helps the Meeting go Down

Do you remember the last donut you had at a company meeting? Were they crusty grocery store donuts or did whomever brought the donuts put some effort into locating a confection of quality? When you are in a position of leadership, culture is not something magical that you pull out of your bag of management tricks, it is you. Therefore, what you do matters, ergo the quality of your donuts matters because that choice reveals something about you.

You are your culture.

> If you bring your people together for an "important meeting" but are too cheap to bring in some snacks, your culture sucks.

> If you put some thought into your meetings but the quality of how you serve your people in that setting is less than the standards you claim that you serve your clients with, your culture is mediocre.

> Conversely, just because you bring the most expensive donuts to a meeting does not instantly mean you have a sweet culture.

I can recall one of my managers telling me, "Be careful about bringing donuts to the meeting, *they* [those entitled employees] will come to expect them." My first thought was something along the lines of, "God forbid our employees come to expect ten dollars worth of dough every time we pulled them into a useless meeting." My second thought was, "Who hurt you? What did the bad man do Teddy?" If you expect that your team will love you just because you bring donuts, you are disconnected with the working people.

> Quality donuts are a small component of proving to yourself and your team that you are not a cheap jerk. Making simple investments in your people and processes will build momentum.

> Quality donuts alone do not solve underlying issues within your culture or leadership. Practice the small things, they go a long way toward making you a more aware person and increasing engagement with your team.

I hate to admit that, at a low point in my career, I had this same corrosive thought one day when I was picking up donuts for my team. I stood outside the local donut shop thinking about some recent poor performance as well as a few disheartening discussions with team members and that friggin sentence crept into my consciousness as though it were a legitimate question. "Should I even be buying donuts for *these people*?"

Thankfully the other voice in my head had some choice words for the gloom-ridden voice with it's inane question. A back street brawl ensued, in my head, and the pessimist was beaten to a pulp. I stepped over the crumpled carcass of my terrible thought and purchased the donuts. We had our meeting, I received a standing ovation by the team and they carried me out upon their shoulders like we had just won the Super Bowl. Only the first item of the previous sentence is true. Business went on and we continued to work out our issues daily.

Business is a battle and if you want to be competitive, donuts won't solve your problems. But they can be a step in the right direction to help you break out of thinking you are stuck in the middle so that you can start blooming where you are planted. Vincent Van Gogh said it beautifully, "Great things are done by a series of small things brought together."

Stuck in the Middle

In business, the term leadership is often used synonymously with management. Authority is tied to symbols, titles and behaviors. Symbols of authority include the badge worn by a police officer. This physical relic displays that the wearer has been sworn in as a member of the law enforcement community. In business we are familiar with titles, they adorn our business cards and our email signatures, informing everyone of our significance.

Behaviors are a bit more interesting, which we will discuss throughout this chapter and throughout the various chapters in this book. I'm excited to hear our collection of authors speak about their experiences with how small things can make a big impact when developing a strong culture.

As far as titles go in the typical organization, the positions of leadership are grouped into three basic tiers of management:

Low-level management

Mid-level management

Top-level management

What is a Mid-Level Manager?

In a large organization this may be one rung above the "common folk" who take the orders and perform the hands-on operations of the business. In these hierarchical structures, a mid-level manager is in a position of leadership that often feels like it has all the responsibility with little overall authority.

In a medium sized company, mid-level management may be synonymous with senior management responsibilities. In the world that I am most familiar with, property restoration (construction), the general manager of a local office is the top-level within that office and yet mid-level when the camera pans out to the broader picture of the corporate structure.

In a small business, the owner may also be the manager and the operator. In most small businesses the organizational chart is rather flat as key members wear multiple hats.

Often the appeal of your role depends on your viewpoint. Mid-level managers feel like those *above* them don't appreciate all that they do for the organization, that top-level management does not respect them. Oddly enough, low-level managers want to reach mid-level management and yet mid-level managers don't believe that they are properly respected by those *below* them. There is a tug-of-war that contributes to the feeling of having to navigate complicated dynamics.

The Power of the Middle

While mid-level management is a challenging position within the structure of a business, the collective responsibility, influence and impact is incalculable. How many people do you know that are in the role of mid-level management? I am sure that the quantity is more than the number of people you know in top-level management. You know a lot of someone's who are in a place where they can impact the culture of an organization via their influence on the people, process, production and progress of that business. I call these *The Four P's of the Blueprint for Success*.

Think about this, according to Wikipedia, "Middle managers have a huge influence on an organisation's development and success as they often have direct control over 80% of an organisation's workforce." If you are a mid-level manager, you likely feel like your influence is difficult to quantify. Mid-level managers have to do an odd dance of both leading and following to an extreme that low-level and top-level managers don't have to contend with.

While we want to discuss the power and impact of small things towards building a strong culture, I think we first have to attack the improper mindset that plagues many in a position of leadership. In the traditional business structure, there is an organizational "leadership ladder." You are either stepping up the ladder or you are being stepped on as someone else rises to the next level of roles and/or responsibilities. If there is at least one someone above you and at least one someone below you, aren't you perpetually in the middle rung of management?

Even if you reach the peak of the ladder, the hallowed C-suite of executive leadership, you still have ownership, investors or a board of directors to answer to. In the case of many businesses in the restoration landscape, corporate mergers and buy-outs mean that you likely answer to a board within as well as a board outside of the board (investors). In many ways, no matter how high you have climbed on the ladder, you will always be the mid-level of something. Embracing the purpose of your planting begins with refusing to be trapped by the ladder mindset.

Your Influence Matters More Than Your Title

When you first set your hand upon the leadership ladder and take that initial step up to the next rung, it feels good. You celebrate with your friends and family. You are finally getting recognized for your hard work. What you soon realize is that when you climb the leadership ladder, at every stride upward you don't have more power and less external inputs. Each tread up the ladder means you have more bosses.

I can remember when I was a project manager and wanted the opportunity to test my ideas as a general manager. I wanted the next level up the ladder. Even though I wanted the opportunity, I knew that as a project manager I had one boss, my general manager. I knew that if I reached the role of general manager, like him, I would be subject to anyone at the corporate office (they preferred to be called "Home Base", because *you know*, we were a "family") that needed something.

The leadership ladder mindset sucks you in. You think that if you climb higher within the corporate structure that you will have more of a say in how things run. You may even be naive enough to think you will receive the *majestic perks* of leadership. As you mature though, I believe you begin to think about what matters to you. If your desire is to make a difference, then you begin to think of where and how this purpose can be most effectively carried out. At some point you wonder if the fight to "make it" is worth the prize(s) at the end of the race.

Wasn't it Jesus who asked, "And what do you benefit if you gain the whole world but lose your own soul?" But he never drove a Tesla, wore a Gucci belt or even owned a pair of socks, so what does he really know about success?

I am thankful for one of my first examples of leadership in a professional setting, a man named Denis.[14] He skillfully demonstrated that one of a manager's key roles is to insulate their people from those things that would demoralize the team or distract them from their purpose. He demonstrated how leading from the middle can result in a positive culture within a department and influence the broader culture. What do I mean by this? I think I can better demonstrate how not to leverage your leadership by sharing an interaction from my career.

I remember a conversation between two persons in a position of leadership. Project manager Talon (we will use this name to protect his real identity), was confronted by the general manager (the "big" boss), we will call him Peter.

"Talon, we are expecting 400 percent margins and yours are at 398. Do you want me to fire you?" Peter, the manager who knows how to inspire his team, chides.

(Note, this is an exaggeration and yet...it isn't. For those of you who are in sales, you know the pressures to produce more with less, year-over-year. If you have 99 projects that are hitting their metrics, you will inevitably be called out for the 1 that isn't.)

"Yeah, I know Peter. It's bugging me as well." Talon responds, as he wipes the orange Dorito dust from his hands to his slacks at 9 o'clock in the morning.

"Well, what are we going to do to get those numbers up?" Peter asks, because he knows that asking the hard questions is what strong leaders do.

"I've been reviewing the numbers and I think it's labor. I think our crew members have been making too many stops to the convenience store and it's adding to their labor costs on my jobs." Talon glows as he knows anytime he blames the crew Peter will bite on that bait.

Talon again wipes his orange fingers across his Kmart specials. (This reference may create a Googling moment for our younger readers. What you should know is that Kmart was not known for selling the highest quality business slacks. This is not a knock on Talon for being unable to purchase nice slacks as Talon was able, Talon chose his fashion like he chose his charm-- discounted.)

"Yeah. Yeah. That's gotta be it. Trips to the convenience store on company time is eating into productivity and taking bites out of our margins." Peter declares, as he both misses the pun as well as the irony of the statement.

If this were a movie, this is where we would show the viewer a recap of when just a few moments earlier Peter saw Talon arrive at work, sans Doritos. Then, like clockwork, because it was his daily habit, Talon departs the office to return a short time later with a fresh bag of Doritos. Talon goes to the convenience store "on company time" and either it doesn't matter or it doesn't impact his productivity. Yet, if an employee at a lower rung in the hierarchy dares to stop for a soda and a snack, it must be the reason the office isn't performing to its potential.

"We ought to have another meeting and really make sure that our crew members understand that stopping at the convenience store on company time is not acceptable." Talon is rolling with the moment. It is unclear if Talon recognizes the hypocrisy or not but he appreciates removing the heat from himself.

Talon is already rehearsing his speech in the glorious conference room that has been set up in his imagination. In this imaginary meeting space, Talon is no holds barred and really able to communicate the depth of his loathing for the crew members. If Talon had better customers and a better crew he could be even better than he already is at his job.

The scene fades out as Talon claws ferociously through the bottom of the empty Doritos bag, straining to grab any last orange speck of his *delicious* morning convenience store treat. Productivity optimization, right?

The Pledge

There is a great meme which first popped up as a mug in my social media feed that states, "This could have been an email." Unfortunately, most people who reach a level of leadership where they have an opportunity to affect real change, defer to ranting emails and meaningless meetings to *really get their point across*. Would you concur with this assessment?

If you are that boss—what happened? Do you remember when you had a terrible boss and you swore, "If I ever get into a position of leadership, I will *never* do that to my people." You took the pledge that so many of us are familiar with and yet, like so many of us, you got there and somehow forgot your roots.

Four quick tips to being a better manager:

1. Don't play the blame game.

2. Have the same set of rules for every employee.

3. Stop with the ranting emails.

4. If you are tempted to have a meeting, don't.

Do you identify with the example of *The Orange Fingers of Hypocrisy* from above? Have you worked with a Talon and/or a Peter? Talons won't take responsibility for their actions; their default is to blame employees and customers for any faults in the projects that they manage. Peters don't see how their inconsistency leads to confusion within the team which is unattractive to good talent. An email is never a good substitute for a face to face discussion when difficult matters must be addressed. If all of your meetings are pointless or result in tirades, they are not helping your cause.

A healthy exercise for anyone in a position of leadership is to reflect on their strengths and weaknesses with regards to The 4 P's:

People. How can I help attract, develop and retain good people?

Process. How can I help to clarify our process and build consistency in our systems?

Production. How can I help to improve our output as a team?

Progress. How can I help to inspire our team to build momentum towards our goals?

When you have orange Dorito dust on your fingers and you point the prickly finger of blame at your team, combined with crappy donuts and endless, pointless meetings, your culture is going to be a negative one. Refusing to play the blame game alone has huge impacts upon how your people interact with each other and your ability as a team to fix the holes in your process. A blame culture holds everyone captive and deepens a sense of being stuck in a toxic environment.

Developing True Accountability

The component that I believe most managers desire to produce is accountability. We hear it in various forms when managers decry the state of the current work force or their need to find better employees. Even though, there again, we have a contradiction, "My workers are terrible, if only I could find better employees then this thing would turn around." Yet, this same manager doesn't take the time to understand the current workforce, dare we say Millennials or Gen Z. So, what do *strong* leaders do? They blame external factors rather than adapting to reality.[1]

Profitability is essential and yet numbers rarely inspire front line employees to operate any differently than they are already predisposed. Executives focus on the bottom line. When there are discrepancies between where the numbers are and where they were projected to be - it's time for accountability. Bad news and responsibility rolls downhill, right? So, the executives talk to the top-level managers and they talk to the mid-level managers and on down to the low-level managers as well as front line employees.

We call this the status quo. When an organization runs according to the status quo, accountability and blame are synonymous. What many miss, is that the beauty and the power of accountability has nothing to do with a manager placing a burden upon their underlings. When a team is clear on the vision and the leadership performs their role to build consistency in the organization, the soil is tilled for accountability to sprout.

Stop phrasing your communication with the team within the context of financial performance. Start thinking through how you as a leader can help your people, process, production and progress. You will gain more ground towards profitability by focusing on The Four P's than you ever will by continuing to hound your team on the numbers.

Keep this in mind, strong accountability has more to do with clarity on the vision and a commitment to the purpose of your organization than it does with employees respecting titles or positions. Leaders at every level must do their part to create clarity and develop consistency if they want to see accountability. There cannot be one set of rules for the managers and another for the technicians. If you believe Doritos are the reason your team is underperforming, the Dorito ban should apply to all, even Talon.

The Dorito Dust Meeting

So, did we ever have the "accountability" meeting that Talon and Peter felt was so important? Yes, we had several of them. They usually followed the results of our end of month or end of quarter reporting. For those who don't know, this is when the corporate office is particularly interested in your local offices operations.

How much revenue did you bring in?

What were your profit margins?

If you're off the mark, what are you going to do to fix these discrepancies going into next quarter?

If you're on the mark, what are you going to do to increase revenues and profits moving forward?

Before you write me off as someone who doesn't understand the necessity of profitability, please take a moment to let me explain. What I am speaking to is the efficacy of how the information is presented so that the goal can be achieved. If you listen and follow what myself and our panel of talented authors are conveying, you will find deeper employee engagement, performance enhancement and a stronger opportunity to collaborate as a team to achieve your goals.

The corporate level of encouragement is always, "Do more with less."

You'll get a brief pat on the back if you're doing it right, then immediately asked what you are going to do to take things higher.

If you are missing the mark, it depends on how frequently, but you'll get the hand on shoulder speech about motivating your team, trimming the fat, increasing sales and, "We know you can do it...but if you don't..."

As a person in a position of leadership, are you honoring your pledge? You swore you wouldn't be like *that* terrible manager from your past, but have you become them? Are you allowing yourself to be trapped in the hamster wheel of ominous perspectives and are regurgitating the ineffective practices you inherited from your dark overlords? You don't have to be stuck in the middle. You can choose to bloom where you are planted.

Four Examples of Leadership Styles

Much of this probably sounds like I am bashing on people in a position of leadership. This is not my intent. My focus is more on asking why we are all part of a status quo cycle of ineffectiveness that we all pledged we would do differently if we ever got into a role of leadership.

The Talon's of the world, either had no positive examples of leadership, or at some point bought into the perspective that looking out for yourself at any cost was the only way to survive. If you have reached a point where your heart is that hard towards others, you may want to consider finding some help. You have some wounds and scars that need to be dealt with for yourself and for your team. Ill intentions repeated will lead to a dark place.

The Peters of the world are the by-product of swearing that they wouldn't be like their worst boss, only to miss that developing positive skills is as important as not repeating those negative traits. Good intentions without guidance or a consistent process lead the same confusion and demotivation that exist with a Talon-like environment. Peters have been hurt; they are trying to do the right thing but they need to keep their focus on clarity and consistency in order to build real accountability.

As I said, one of my first managers, Denis, demonstrated that a manager's role is to insulate their team from those things that will distract them from their purpose or suck the wind out of their sails. The Denis's of the world are confident in who they are; they know their strengths as well as their weaknesses. As such, they are able to assist their team members to find their strengths and contribute those facets to the growth of the team. When you embrace your identity and live your purpose, like a Denis, you find ways to bridge the gap between what those further up the ladder want to see from the team and what needs to be done at the local level.

To the Sharons of the world (see Chapter *Encouragement to Organizations*), who have built a business from the ground up and continue to have a direct hand in operations, what an accomplishment! Whether you feel like things are going well or you're constantly pulling your hair out, take a moment to give yourself credit for daring to follow your instincts and building something. If you need to get things back on course, join the club, you are in good company and we are rooting for you. Keep taking small steps in the right direction and celebrate your progress in the process.

Small Changes Make a Big Difference

The next time something happens and you are tempted to point the orange finger of blame, stop and ask yourself, "What can we do that will produce the best long term result?" This is a complex question as each situation is unique. I can assure you, blame is not the answer. Even if you are able to pin the blame on one person, does doing this solve your broader issue?

I arrived at an assignment where my role was described as, "Elevating our training program so that our technicians could take more ownership for their roles." According to the department head (Talon) and the general manager (Peter), the last operations manager had failed to develop their team. I had heard early on that if they will blame the last guy for something, they will blame you for it. I asked in the interview if it was only this prior manager's fault and the two assured me they held blame as well.

When I arrived in the team meeting area I noticed a large white board with names, dates and descriptions on it.

I asked the team, "What is this?"

They replied, "It's the Naughty Board."

I laughed.

They did not.

I asked, "For what?"

"Whenever we break something our name goes on the board." A team member responded, looking quizzically at me--as though I was asking an odd question.

"You're joking?"

"Nope."

"Take it down," I instructed.

Now they looked scared, "You'll have to ask Talon about that."

"Is he the one who made this board?" I asked.

"That's correct," another team member responded.

I grabbed a screw gun, took the board down, and had a lot of fun breaking it into several smaller pieces so that it could not ever be reused.

The Destruction of the Naughty Board

I couldn't believe it and yet I would soon learn this was only the beginning. The Naughty Board is where it belongs, in the bottom of a rotting pile of trash in some landfill. If you're still wondership what this was, let me explain. In property restoration we often deal with fire damaged homes. Before we can address the needs of the structure, one of the things that we must do is to inventory and pack out all of the belongings of the homeowner.

Contents inventory and pack out is a tedious process. It requires training on a regular basis for items such as how to properly pack a box, how to document pre-loss conditions, proper labeling of items and ensuring that your inventory is thorough. Training is the responsibility of the leadership team. If you are in a position of leadership it is your job to create clarity in your process before you expect consistency from your production team.

Remember, I was hired because the training and development was lacking. Talon felt his best input for the team was not in becoming engaged in the hands on training but developing a stupid board that blasted anyone who made a mistake. I have always trained my teams, mistakes happen, we can deal with mistakes. What makes things very difficult is if you hide your mistakes.

In the case of packing out a customer's home, things break. As outlined in the closing of *Encouragement to Growth Minded Professionals*, I would constantly tell my team in training and as we on-boarded new employees, if you hide a mistake I cannot help you. If you tell me about a mistake we can work together to find a solution. I learned from Denis that the worst thing for a leader is to be blindsided. If you break something, I want to know about it immediately. If you notify me we can look for a replacement and discuss the item with the owner rather than them coming home to find it.

How do you Respond When the Worst Happens?

One negative example which demonstrates this point perfectly comes to mind. We had a project where a painting subcontractor was onsite. I get a call from my assistant that a customer is upset because something was broken--not a big deal. The problem was how the customer discovered this broken item. Thankfully the customer was a reasonable person, they said, "It's just a cheap lamp from Walmart, I could have picked one up on my way home if I knew it was broken. What I don't understand is why they shoved it behind the couch." It was a great training moment for our team as we were able to get the lamp details, purchase it and have it back onsite by the next morning.

On the other hand, we had a project where the customer had several glass figurines and beautiful chinaware. There was one case that was of particular importance to her as the collection had come from someone special and was only available in Europe. We did the walk through with the customer to identify these items. We did a walk through with our contents team and discussed that glass case in particular. We had notes on the paperwork and the site lead was aware of the importance of the items in that case.

I received *the call* from the site lead, "I don't know how to tell you this, I feel so bad..." Oh no, "Let me guess, something was broken in that case?" The site lead was nearly in tears, "Yes. We were being so delicate but the figures were stuck to the glass and when we pulled gently the shelf came loose and shattered the shelf below." Not the call you want to receive. We all were heart sunk.

We rushed to the site and confirmed the details. Thankfully the shelves below had been emptied successfully and I don't recall but it ended up being 1 or 2 items that were broken in addition to the shelves in the case. I had to make the call to the customer.

I explained the situation and that we make no excuses for breaking her items, especially the items that meant the most to her. Thankfully she had been onsite on a few occasions with our contents crew and had observed how careful they were being with her items. She wasn't happy but she was confident in our crew and we forwarded all of the information from the site to the insurance company to assist with replacing the damaged items.

Reinforcing Your Culture one Response at a Time

As soon as I got back to the office I constructed my own naughty board by using my utility knife to carve the names of those employees into our office wall.

No, that's not true. We did what we always did, at our next team huddle we discussed what happened and what we learned from the experience. Taking the Naughty Board down was only one step in the process. I continued to discuss and reinforce our new approach to training, working as a team and owning our setbacks as a purpose driven group.

We never saw the Naughty Board again but it took consistent reinforcement in training and in my responses to incidents in order to build an environment where the team trusted me by sharing critical things such as mistakes made. I don't believe you can prevent all mistakes as a manager but you can create a culture where our setbacks don't define our performance and open the floor for collaboration by removing barriers.

When our team members can connect and collaborate, they can conquer. Mechanisms of fear, such as the Naughty Board, reduce your ability to build transparency and collaboration. As a person in a position of leadership you have to walk what you talk, train consistently for the results that you want to see and allow accountability to build from within your team. If you are not authentic, you don't train and you force a false culture, you will die a painful death.

The Next Step is Yours

At some point you realize the difference between being stuck and being planted is a matter of perspective. Remember, Peters mean well but because they don't set a clear and positive vision, they usually repeat the atmosphere and results of those negative managers they swore they would never become. Being a Denis means knowing your strengths and working to help others understand and operate from theirs. You will be much happier as a Denis and so will your team.

If you are in a position of leadership and you have a Talon on your team, you need to have some hard conversations with clear steps of improvement. If you can't identify a Talon on your team, you may be that person. If you have rooted those individuals out you will need to remain intentional about not bringing that type of person in or allowing those mannerisms to take root in your team. The Sharons of the world have a beautiful opportunity to recognize that empowering people is good for your business, your team and for you.

Wherever you are, you are in the middle of something. In business, you can choose to be stuck in mid-level management hell, which I hope I have demonstrated is a construct of the mind rather than a by-product of your position. You can be *stuck* or you can be *planted*. Water your mindset, give it some sunlight and tend to the soil. When you start to bloom, take that positivity and help others to do the same.

Buy some nice donuts for your team, wash the orange off of your fingers, walk away from the blame game and tear down your Naughty Board. Continue to do small things to impact your culture and enjoy the progress in the process.

CHAPTER 7

Practice What You Preach

By Jeremy Watkin

G rowing up in the home of a minister, I was quite familiar with the saying, "Practice what you preach." After all, what do you call a preacher who implores their congregation to live one way while doing the exact opposite in their personal life? That's right, a hypocrite.

It's with that moral framework that I felt I could pass judgement on an organization for supplying the bathrooms, where 95% of their slightly-above-minimum-wage workforce worked, with the cheap sand, I mean toilet paper. While the executive office was supplied with the cushy, two-ply stuff—yes, I primarily got to use the latter.

It's easy to pass judgement when organizations tout their flat structure and fair treatment of all employees when, all the while, the bulk of their workforce walks around the office like they commuted to work on a horse.

Coming to terms with my own hypocrisy

The reality is that there's hypocrisy all over the place, but the goal of this chapter isn't to point out the hypocrisy in others. Let me share a bit about my story.

It was 2012 and I had a little more than a decade worth of experience in customer service, and at the time I was managing a customer service team. I was in the airport in Salt Lake City, Utah waiting on some food I ordered when I witnessed the true impact of a terrible customer experience.

To make a long story short, a customer tried to order coffee from one completely disengaged employee who instructed the customer to proceed to the cash register. When the customer proceeded to order coffee from the cashier, she learned that the restaurant didn't serve coffee. They didn't even have a coffee maker! It was awfully nice of the first employee to withhold that particular detail, wasn't it?. Understandably, the customer was livid and stormed out of the restaurant, leaving her other items behind.

It may go without saying that any time a customer is misled in this way, there's a pretty good chance they'll be upset. This was a perfect visual of the customer walking out and never coming back.

Realizing that I had some experience in this space, I immediately started a blog about customer service with the sole purpose of observing both good and bad customer experiences and extracting valuable lessons to share with my team — and the Internet, if they cared to read about them.

At the time I thought this blog would be an opportunity to judge others and determine if their work in customer experience was good or bad. What I didn't bargain for was the period of deep introspection that resulted from this observational and blogging exercise followed by the illumination into all of the areas where I didn't measure up as a customer service professional and leader. The blog became instant accountability for me to begin practicing what I was preaching. I quickly realized that I was a hypocrite.

As I ponder the full extent of my hypocrisy, I'll use the balance of this chapter to share some of the most profound lessons I've learned as I strive to be a practice-what-you-preach leader.

Lesson 1: Don't Preach it Until you Practice it Yourself

How many times have you browsed job postings and come across companies that describe their ideal candidate as someone who can multitask? I've been guilty of putting that in job postings as a hiring manager, and worse, I have actually asked my employees to multitask. That was until I realized firsthand that multitasking is impossible and any attempts lead to customer aggravation and put employees on the fast track to burnout.

Early in my customer service career, our company handled calls and emails from customers but, at some point, decided to add live chat as an option. We had a small team and demand for the channel was low, so I asked our team to handle at least one chat while also taking phone calls — more if they weren't on the phone. It seemed like a reasonable request given that they already responded to emails in between calls.

For several months the team was wildly inconsistent in their handling of chats so I ratcheted up the pressure. I celebrated those couple people who knocked it out of the park and implored the bottom performers to improve.

It wasn't until one fateful Saturday when I covered a shift for a team member who was out sick that I realized the error of my ways. In an effort to prove that chats and calls could be handled simultaneously, I signed into both systems. How hard could it be? Well, moments later my question was answered and I quickly learned that it was actually impossible to handle both chats and calls at the same time. As I spoke to one customer, I tried simultaneously to type a response to another customer in the chat and completely mixed up the two conversations.

What I was requiring of my team was unreasonable, and it wasn't until I tried it for myself, that I was able to experience just how unreasonable it was. Another way to describe this important lesson is to never require someone to do that which you're not willing to do yourself.

Lesson 2: Admit When Your Words and Actions are Incongruent

As a leader, I often spent much of my day in meetings and interacting with employees. This often left the evening for catching up on email and other busy work. Meanwhile, I encouraged my team to enjoy their nights and weekends off and not worry about working. I said things like, "Don't be a hero. The work will still be here in the morning."

On one particular evening I was doing some work when I came across an issue where I thought one of my employees could have handled something better. Without thinking, I emailed her to inquire about the situation. Upon checking my email early the next morning, I found a fairly distressed response from her.

Realizing that my email had a negative impact on her when she was supposed to be enjoying her time off, I quickly wrote her back and apologized for my handling of the situation. I told her it was not a big deal, and that it could wait until Monday. As it turned out, I misunderstood and she had handled the situation perfectly.

As a leader, I was valiantly encouraging my employees to relax when not at work but then sending them work to do by emailing them. This incongruity between my words and actions communicated that, even though I said they didn't need to work, my actions indicated the exact opposite.

No leader is perfect, as much as we'd like to think we are. Sooner or later you will become aware of a blind spots in your leadership style — inconsistencies between your words and actions. Rest assured that this is completely normal! The key here is that when blind spots come to light, you recognize them, admit fault, and commit to improving.

Lesson 3: Integrity is Everything

Let's talk about integrity and where I found myself falling short as a leader. Before diving into my story, let's define it. Integrity is doing what's right, even when no one is watching.

Early on in my career in customer service, before becoming a manager, I had a few subtle lapses in integrity. The first were the multiple instances where I would be working with a customer, they had a question, and I didn't know the answer. Knowing it was a whole lot of work to find an answer, I'd just subtly tell the customer I couldn't help them and then hope they'd accept that and go away. And there was a good chance the next time they called, one of my coworkers would have to deal with the customer instead of me. I didn't put forth my best effort to take care of the customer and I knew it.

Then there were those calls where I was working at home and

perhaps the customer was rude, slow, or lacking in computer savvy. Or perhaps it was me who was hangry and ready for my shift to end. Regardless of the excuse, I was a complete jerk, sometimes even yelling — and there's no excuse for unprofessional behavior.

It was wrong and I knew it. You know how I knew it? Because when the customer asked to speak with my boss, my tone changed and I instantly became more helpful.

I can remember occasions where new team members came to me with their twentieth question of the day and I told them to buzz off. Or in other cases I might have answered their question but avoided eye contact or acted like they were inconveniencing me. After all, I was busy with "managerial stuff" and couldn't be bothered with questions from the people I was managing. It really wasn't a good look on me.

Admittedly, any profession where you work with people all day long and are required to solve complex problems, will test your patience. But I realized that if I was going to write a blog about great customer service and set a high standard for my team, I needed to raise the bar for myself as well. That's what integrity is all about.

Lesson 4: Stop passing the buck

The expression, "The buck stops here" was made famous by President Harry S. Truman, but it actually originated in the game of poker where a knife with a buckhorn handle was passed around to indicate whose turn it was to deal. Players who didn't want to deal could "pass the buck" to the next person.

"The buck stops here" is an admission of ownership and an acceptance of responsibility to be the person to make a decision or solve a problem rather than passing it to someone else. I proved to be great at passing the buck when I was less than helpful with a customer hoping they'd be connected with one of my coworkers the next time they called. I also passed the buck when I chose to show aggravation toward a colleague or a customer rather than digging in and solving their issue.

As I began aiming to practice what I preached, I became keenly aware of the fact that once a call escalated to me or a colleague came asking for help, there weren't many other places to send them. My boss certainly didn't want to talk to customers. That's why he hired me and promoted me into leadership. This meant that, for better or for worse, I was committed. It was a take-ownership-of-the-situation-and-solve-the-problem-or-bust sort of thing.

In these situations, I learned that attitude is everything. A negative attitude certainly makes the entire experience more painful. Realizing that I could instead choose a positive attitude, solving problems for customers and employees got easier. As I said earlier, working with people all day is still incredibly hard work, but the challenge of turning difficult situations around actually became fun.

As you aim to practice what you preach, you may find that you need to be more positive, adopting a buck stops here mindset. Here are three tools that have helped me immensely.

1. Don't be Afraid to Learn Something New

It's easy and tempting to pass the buck when we don't know the answer. In the case of an employee asking for help, just pretend you're too busy with managerial duties and leave them to find another way, right? Stopping the buck doesn't automatically mean that you will know all of the answers. But you can commit to learning alongside the person asking the question. What a great way to support both your team and your customers.

2. Become Intelligent About Your Emotions

Part of accepting the buck requires stepping back and assessing how we feel about a situation. While it would be nice to plan out every aspect of our workday, things rarely follow the plan when you're working with people. Interruptions are a given.

Emotionally intelligent leaders are able to recognize their emotional response to adverse circumstances. Frustration and impatience are normal feelings that can quickly cascade into a negative mindset. The first step in mastering those negative emotions is recognizing their existence. Once you recognize them for what they are, you can choose your response. With practice, I'm getting better at staying positive and focused on the solution—I'm not sure I'll ever be done practicing this one.

3. Take Complete Ownership

Taking ownership of the situation means there's no escape hatch. There's no more hoping problems (AKA customers and employees) will magically disappear. Leaders who take ownership commit to finding a solution and don't relinquish ownership until they've either solved the problem, or someone better suited to own it takes over.

The Results

Put simply, this shift to practicing what I preach has been life changing for me as a manager, customer service professional, and human being. But I fear I've done enough preaching and it's time to talk about the results of this practice. There are a couple stories that come to mind that illustrate the impact to both the customers I was serving and the team I was managing.

First a customer story. I recall a time when I spoke with an upset customer, and rather than becoming impatient, I took the time to listen and learn. The result was a fascinating conversation where I got to see our service from her perspective. I ended up with a list several bullet points deep of ways we could improve our service.

After our conversation, I sent the customer a thank you note expressing my appreciation for the fact that she took time out of her busy day to give us her honest feedback. Customers do not have to do this and their feedback is extremely valuable. Later she completed a customer satisfaction survey and this is the comment she left:

> After many frustrating experiences setting up my service, management has been SUPERIOR in listening and making corrections. Would you believe a thank you note from a supervisor for my suggestions? The company's procedures for new customers still need work but I am encouraged by the bend over backwards attitude of the real live people who quickly respond to customer issues. Color me hopeful.

I don't share this story with you to toot my own horn but to tell you that this *practice what you preach* stuff really works. It's a great way to get and keep (attract and retain) customers.

One more story — this time from the team I managed. Imagine my shock and horror when I arrived at work one Boss's Day to find that my entire team was wearing shirts with my face on them that read "I Love My Boss." Did I mention that my face was superimposed on the body of Miley Cyrus on a wrecking ball? I'll leave the rest to your imagination.

It also came to my attention that a member of my team hijacked my blog and wrote a post about me. Here's an excerpt:

Yes he is the Director, but he also stays in the support loop by helping out customers. Jeremy works on emailing those who need assistance, handles direct calls with customers, and if need be will make himself available to do an in house support visit for those customers in the area. He also listens to the customer and takes their feedback to heart. He's always looking for ways to develop and enhance the customer experience.

In regards to helping our team, if we have a question, his door is always open. He makes himself available to everyone in our office, not just support staff, to help with a variety of tasks and questions. If he doesn't have the answer you need he'll point you in the right direction.

Does this sound like the same manager who lost his cool with employees and customers? This is proof positive that if I can choose to practice what I preach, so can you.

CHAPTER 8

A Poem About Culture

By Elan Pasmanick

Tim once was a warehouse manager

He was not at all an amateur

He knew exactly what was his mission

And kept the warehouse in sparkling condition

The equipment and other materials were neatly kept

Always the bathroom clean and the floor swept

Exhausted he was because nobody gave him a hand

And felt that he's drawing in quicksand

So slowly he just stopped giving a damn

To all he started looking like a big sham

The manager wanted him to fire

To the owner he came, "We need Tim to retire!"

The owner asked, "What is the big trouble?"

"His head is in space like the telescope Hubble!

The goods he is not anymore supplying,

He has stopped even trying!"

The owner said, "I have a notion that Tim
just needs a promotion.

I now declare that Tim is in charge

Of all in the warehouse small and large,

From Tim for equipment you'll ask

Politely after wearing a face mask,

And the men will take turns with the cleaning

To teach some respect to the warehouse keeping."

Tim once again excelled in his job

And never again acted like a slob.

*If you want to get more context for Elan's unique perspectives observing skilled trades organizations from a unique viewpoint repairing equipment in their warehouses, you can listen to The DYOJO Podcast Episode 8 - *Extending the Life of Your Restoration Equipment*.

PART 2:

*How Small Things   Under-
mine Your Culture*

CHAPTER 9

*Can Diversity, Equity & Inclusion
Initiatives Really Affect
Company Culture?*

By Dr. Leroy D. Nunery II

Over the last few years, I've been spending a substantial amount of time reading through multiple studies on the issues of Diversity, Equity, and Inclusion (DEI). It's not surprising that most, if not all, of the studies highlight the paucity of representation of "different" or "diverse" individuals (as identified by racial, ethnic, religious, gender preference, etc.) in C-suite, senior and/or middle management ranks. By and large, the studies point out that underrepresentation, particularly in the insurance industry, is due to the same factors I uncovered when I wrote *The Journey of African American Insurance Professionals* [15]: Lacks of exposure, networking opportunities, and experience become substantial obstacles for most "diverse" professionals. Several companies struggle with how to overcome these prevailing obstacles. Whose issue is it, and who is responsible for resolving those obstacles:

The individual?
The company?
Society?

Current Approaches to Diversity and Inclusion

Some organizations try to address the obstacles by creating slates of candidates that have minorities on them, similar to the Rooney Rule in the National Football League. As described by the NFL,

"The Rooney Rule, named after the late former Pittsburgh Steelers owner and chairman of the league's diversity committee, Dan Rooney, was adopted in 2003 as a formal policy requiring every team with a head coaching vacancy to interview at least one or more diverse candidates. In 2009, the Rooney Rule was expanded to include general manager jobs and equivalent front office positions."[16]

Other companies try to present a diverse image through their advertising, e.g., using multiracial actors to sell their products, seemingly hoping that customers will perceive that the company is welcoming, warm, and current with demographic trends. *Fast Company* magazine reported on a 2019 study[17] from Heat, which looked at ads for 50 brands from the Top 200 media spenders, across eight industries. Dr. William O'Barr, a Duke University professor of anthropology, and Dr. Kevin Thomas, a University of Texas at Austin advertising professor, were consulted to analyze the intersection of diversity and advertising. The key metrics they identified included:

> *Showcasing diversity in primary roles (speaking roles versus background)*

> *Illustrating diverse characters in positions of power (buying a burger versus selling the burger)*

> *Contrasting stereotypical roles (woman cooking versus woman pursuing a career)*

The research team discovered that:

> *94% of the brands in the study had at least one occurrence of women in a primary role*

> *57% of which were in positions of power, but even half of those roles still featured a stereotypical element like empathetic*

mom, devoted wife, or boy-focused girl.

Also, 92% of the brands studied had at least one occurrence of a person of color in a primary role, but only 15% of those were culturally diverse.

It was also brought to light that representation for the LGBTQ+ community as well as depictions of individuals with a disability were lacking in mainstream advertising.

Less than 1% of ads represented a character who would identify as LGBTQ+.

Despite one in four American adults living with some type of disability, again, less than 1% of the ads featured a character with one.

90% of ads didn't include people of lower socioeconomic backgrounds.

And yet others have CEOs and other representatives who regularly and proudly present policy platforms that espouse their desire for inclusion and equity. Notably, the CEO Action for Diversity & Inclusion™ is the largest CEO-driven business commitment to advance diversity and inclusion within the workplace. This commitment is driven by a realization that addressing diversity and inclusion is not a competitive issue, but a societal issue. Recognizing that change starts at the executive level, more than 900 CEOs of the world's leading companies and business organizations, are leveraging their individual and collective voices to advance diversity and inclusion in the workplace[18].

The Results?

Despite these well-conceived and broadly advertised initiatives, it's difficult to see tangible results. The NFL's Rooney Rule was celebrated as a DEI milestone because of the league's visibility and popularity, and yet in 2020, while "59 percent of players are black and 70 percent are nonwhite, according to

The Institute For Diversity And Ethics In Sport (TIDES), only 12.5 percent of regular-season NFL games this past season were coached by people of color, a share that will hold steady to start the 2020 season."[19]

In the corporate section, there are only four Black CEOs of Fortune 500 companies (Merck, TIAA, Tapestry, Lowe's), according to Korn Ferry's recent study, "The Black P&L Leader: Insights and Lessons from Senior Black P&L leaders in Corporate America."[20] Despite overwhelming evidence that America's demographics are, and will change, it is abundantly clear that having "different" faces on a television commercial, or making sure that an interview slate has some "pepper mixed in with the salt", hasn't really or substantially changed the status quo.

To be sure, the insurance industry's management ranks reflect the broader underrepresentation problem, being predominantly homogeneous (read white, male, straight). So, although DEI efforts are pronounced and underway, the outcomes are remarkably unremarkable. In "An Analysis of Diversity and Inclusion in the Insurance Industry[21]", written by Terrance J. Evans on the American Bar Association's website, the facts reflect the lack of remarkability in the demographics in mutual insurance companies:

> 93% of executive leadership is white
> 1% black
> 2% Asian
> 3% Hispanic
> 1% other

The "real" diversity, i.e., a broader and mixture of gender, race, ethnicity, etc., is found at the professional, administrative and trainee levels.

In conducting research for The Journey Study, which included interviews with 25 seasoned (over 10 years) African American insurance professionals, I learned that many carriers and agencies struggle to fully embrace or implement the initiatives. These interviewees were sometimes told that they "didn't fit " within a company's culture, or "weren't ready" for the next promotion (even though they had substantially greater experience than a majority colleague who eventually go the promotion), or as in one case, learned that a senior manager felt that the individual didn't "understand how we operate". These seemingly subtle but nonetheless concrete messages convey a sense that no matter one's education, technical competencies, or readiness, the goals of diversity and inclusion are elusive.

What's the Answer?

I am often asked, "Who's doing it well?", i.e., are there any insurance companies that seem to have a handle on correcting for the inequities. I find that to be an intriguing question, as if there is a specific prescription or remedy for a long standing, historical problem, almost like writing a policy against the risk of that issue. Since writing The Journey Study, I've not found any one company which seems to "have it all figured out". Instead, there are some solutions that appear to be working for individual organizations, and it would be foolish to assume that "one size would fit all" (like umbrella policy coverage).

Similar to the customized risk management solutions that the insurers offer their clients--based upon the client's needs, goals, and profiles--I think each company should look deep inside and find DEI solutions that will optimize the outcomes for the respective firm. For example, The Hartford has been recognized by Forbes magazine, the Bloomberg Financial Services Gender-Equity Index, the Human Rights Campaign Foundation, and others for its DEI multi-point strategy, which includes the formation of multiple Employee Resource Groups (for Mature Professionals, FlexAbilities, and Military Community), supplier diversity programs, holding forums on courageous conversations, and most importantly, tying DEI initiatives to business performance.

A huge question that confronts several insurance companies--given the pending shortfall of incoming talent--is whether or not their leaders really want to solve the problem. Here are critical questions that I ask in my travels:

> Is there shared responsibility and accountability throughout the organization for achieving DEI goals?

> Are all managers and leaders expected to adhere to the organization's DEI initiatives?

> Even if there a diverse set of candidates are presented, how often are managers allowed to "go with the familiar" and go unchallenged for that choice?

> How often does the company present its DEI results (e.g., number of hires, retention rates, new markets tapped, etc.)?

> Would appointing a D&I Officer help to move the needle, and if it does, will that D&I officer have the power and/or influence to create change within the organization?

I believe that there are clear advantages for an organization to undertake the challenges of achieving greater equity because not only will talent flow to that company, but also because firms that embrace and implement gender or ethnic diversity initiatives have demonstrably better profitability, as reported in two related studies called Diversity Matters I (2014) and II (2017) by McKinsey & Co. The most gender diverse firms experienced:

> 15% stronger Earnings Before Interest and Taxes (EBIT) in 2014 than their industry counterparts

> 22% higher EBIT in 2017

Likewise, the most ethnically diverse firms experienced 35% stronger EBIT in 2014 and 2017 than industry counterparts. The bottom line is that diversity can be a driver for the business.

What Can You Do?

There remains a prevailing question around why an organization would undertake the challenge. Until "why" is posed and answered, underrepresentation will continue. Bringing "diverse" people on board only solves part of the problem; there has to be a commitment from leaders--throughout the organization--to see the disadvantages of having homogeneous, monolithic cultures. A few easy steps to take are:

> Becoming an executive sponsor for and/or regular participant in an ERG;

> Holding roundtable discussions with others whose cultures and communities that are different than their own, and encouraging dialogue;

> Report out the results of DEI initiatives, such as recruiting, hiring, and promotions; or,

> Inquiring if company advertisements that show a wonderfully mixed group of happy customers are really working to attract new customers from those respective groups.

Without an expressed--and demonstrated dedication to equity from the top of an organization, an explicit integration of DEI initiatives into the organization's business strategy, and a personal responsibility to make cultural change--all of the advertisements in the world won't matter. It goes beyond slogans or commercials that are even making a magazine's top 100 list for being a "best employer". If leaders can articulate why they feel personally bound to achieve broader diversity and inclusion, and are willing to commit to the work, then the future will be exceptionally brighter.

CHAPTER 10

*Eliminating Mixed Messages
in Your Culture*

By Andrew McCabe

Several years ago, I found myself in an organization with a broken culture. Taken individually, the examples I will cite are not necessarily indicative of a "bad" or toxic culture. But as a whole, they paint a picture of a company which had lost its purpose.

In early 2014, I accepted a management position with a franchise property restoration company in Bend, Oregon. By restoration I am referring to an organization that works with insurance companies to help home and business owners who have experienced damages such as water or fire at their property. I was looking for a fresh start in a new town. Bend had always been one of our wishlist towns. We sold our home in Portland and began all the preparations to begin our lives again.

The house sold in June, and we found a great place in Bend, moving just in time for Independence Day celebrations. I started work the following Monday.

I could tell right away that something wasn't quite right.

I arrived to learn that two water techs had quit the previous week, and another lead tech had given her 2-week notice. That amounted to half of the mitigation department staff. No amount of damage control over the next week was going to change her mind.

Before she left the company, I was able to speak with her. There was a harassment situation with another water tech which had gone unresolved for some time. She didn't feel heard, understood, or safe, so she found a job with a competitor across town.

Other female technicians told me not to schedule the offending technician with them; they refused to work with him. In my heart I knew the right course of action - this guy had to go.

Yet, when I raised the issue with the General Manager, I was told this was "simply a personality conflict." I asked to see the employee's HR discipline records. There were none. A female employee had complained to her manager regarding harrassment, and no record had been made of it. No email, no note in either file.

The instigating technician was seen as a high performing (read: money-making) employee. He was an Army veteran as well, which put him in a different light because my boss had a long military career before coming to the civilian side. I got the distinct feeling that management had decided the situation was a non-issue and that production came first.

If I was allowed to let the technician go, it would potentially disrupt production (cash flow). It was also expressed to me that he would sue the company for wrongful termination if fired. In spite of the company's overly cautious approach to this situation, he quit three months later...and he still sued the company for wrongful termination.

When we accept a toxic person in our ranks, we invite toxicity into our organizations. We also send an unambiguous signal to the rest of those under our care: as long as we're making money, you don't matter.

When people don't feel safe at work, their engagement suffers. When we accept poor behavior (and failing to address it is the same as accepting it), we encourage more of the same. When a toxic personality is allowed to persist, we destroy any culture we might have had. Companies that recognize these truths and act on them are building a stronger culture on a daily basis. Toxic personalities are a drag on culture and profits. It should be no surprise that a strong culture leads to strong profits.

Following Through on Your Ethics

Early in my career, I had the opportunity to work with a company which had a strong culture. Everyone seemed to have that innate sense of what the organization stood for.

When decisions were made, there was a certain clarity and speed by which they were made that only comes from people who are empowered and part of a team. Situations weren't viewed as "right" or "wrong", but rather "is this right *for us* or not?"

We were very clear on who our clients were as well as our target market. There were no apologies made for intentionally turning away certain opportunities simply because they didn't fit who we were.

For example, we didn't market to insurance adjusters--like the majority of the restoration industry at the time. We didn't spend time "wining and dining" at golf tournaments and such, because we knew who our customers were--and they weren't insurance companies.

The company focused religiously on the commercial real estate and multi-family residential markets. The entire organization was geared for large-scale emergency response and the ensuing large loss repairs. They employed an entire department whose sole purpose was to identify emergencies across five states and dispatch local responders any time day or night.

The "chasing" business model was frowned upon by some in our industry. People called us ambulance chasers, believing that we were preying on folks who were at their most vulnerable. I honestly didn't completely buy into the concept right away. My view was tainted by what I had heard from others over the years.

Early on I spent time with our resident "chaser", the one responsible for heading out in the middle of the night and weekends, responding to major fire losses. I quickly began to see the truth of what my company was doing.

He was being a genuine resource to the local community. The vast majority of people who suffer major losses have no idea how to respond. Home and business owners don't have a real plan in place most of the time. My company entered this chaos with actionable advice and the knowledge to respond to tragedy with a process. This service mindset won many jobs that would have otherwise gone to what our industry calls the "program" vendors.

For those reading this book who aren't familiar with the insurance claims process as it relates to restoring your home or business, a program vendor is synonymous with a "preferred" vendor. In most states the insurance policy holder has the option to choose the contractor they want to use to assist them with their claim. But many insurance carriers will try to encourage, some more forcefully than others, to use restoration contractors who are members of their preferred vendor network; those who go along with the "program".

While some people look down on contractors who "chase" the work, what other options are there for contractors who remain independent of the "program"? For our organization, if we were going to acquire work and help clients with their damages, we had to distinguish ourselves with our service model. Serving with honesty and integrity was the key. Our "chasers" never lied or made unrealistic promises in order to win the business; they simply showed up consistently and helped our clients with heart.

Sustaining this sort of culture takes more than deploying honesty and integrity when dealing with clients and those outside the organization. It is critical that these same values are also applied internally.

After a short lived stint as an Operations Manager in Arizona, I was charged with running a smaller branch operation in my home state in 2008. "Charged with" is probably too strong; but I jumped at the chance to move away from the Phoenix area.

With revenues South of $5 million, this new office was one of the smallest branch offices in the larger organization. But at the ripe age of 33 years old, it felt gigantic to me. I was in charge of a team of restoration professionals, most of whom had at least a decade more experience than I did.

One of these more experienced folks was a senior project manager named "Joe", whom I had met before while we were both working for other restoration companies. He was well-liked in our local market and was responsible for the lion's share of my new office's annual revenue. I wasn't sure why he wasn't offered the General Manager's position instead of me.

Right away I started to see hints of why he wasn't. It started, and ended, with his expense reports.

As with a lot of project managers/estimators in our industry, we were expected to market to potential clients and treat our existing clients. This would often include excursions such as taking them out for meals, meeting up for happy hour, buying rounds of golf, and the like were all standard practice. It was an expected part of the job to spend time outside of work trying to build your personal book of business.

When it would come time to review expense reports I would see the usual things: dinner with so-and-so, golf at such-and-such association, supplies for XYZ project. All of these were very normal and usually approved without question. But with Joe, there were these frequent pizza purchases.

It was actually the second time I had seen it that I brought it up to him. Every other Friday or so, there would be a charge at Figaro's Pizza for $13 around 4:30pm.

"I must have grabbed the wrong card," was his answer. I accepted it without much thought. I asked myself, what's thirteen bucks in the grand scheme of things? Then I saw it again: pizza on Friday afternoon from a restaurant that was on his way home. He was regularly treating his family to pizza on the company dime.

Once again, I did nothing. Why didn't he deserve a pizza for all his hard work? Lord knows we all spend nights and weekends in disaster situations for little, if any, recompense. It's one of the unspoken rules: any time and anywhere, restorers respond in force. You would be hard pressed to find a professional in the property restoration industry who doesn't have a war story about pulling all-nighters during CAT events only to show up at 7am sharp for work the next day?

As a sidenote, CAT is short for catastrophic events. On a national scale, hurricanes are CAT events that pull significant resources to a region impacted by a sudden natural disaster. On a regional scale, extreme cold weather can lead to catastrophic conditions such as pipes bursting and ice dams. On a local scale, a large loss, such as a flood at college or a fire in a large commercial building may be considered a CAT event for the teams responding to these events.

The truth was, Joe felt he was untitled to a little something extra. I didn't call him out those first two incidents, because I did too. We had both succumbed to what Simon Sinek calls *Ethical Fading*.

Not long after, I received a call from our CFO. There was a recurring charge on Joe's credit card that didn't look right. I looked into these discrepancies and, at first, I brushed it off. It turns out, the charge in question was for a utility bill. I had observed the charge when approving the expense report but dismissed it as job related.

Joe had a long-term restoration project in progress. During the course of repairs, the owner had stopped paying their utility bills, and the power had been shut off. Our crews needed electricity and water to continue their work, so Joe naturally called in to have the charges applied to his company credit card to keep things moving. This wasn't uncommon and we would recover our expenses into our final supplemental invoice.

Or so I thought.

"That would make sense," the CFO told me patiently, "Except the service address is for Joe's house."

What I didn't know is that my CFO had done some digging of her own. She called the municipality listed on the charge and got them to reveal the address for which our company card had been used. They confirmed that it was Joe's alright. She emailed me a copy of the statement.

I knew what I had to do, but to stall, I called the president of the company.

"Andy, I think you know what you have to do," was his somber advice.

Yes, I did.

I took Joe's phone, keys, and credit card and had someone drive him home. What did he say in his defense? The same response as before, "I must have grabbed the wrong card." I knew it was the right thing to do but it was still one of the hardest things I've ever done.

In retrospect, there had been a number of ethical infractions which I had brushed off. My gut had been telling me something was not quite right for some time. I just didn't want to hear it.

I believe that, had I handled the pizza situation with better leadership and firm boundaries, that Joe wouldn't have been fired. I failed him, and my company, by not upholding these standards.

The president had seen the same thing, and I'll never forget what he told me when I saw him next. "Andy," he said, "I've never fired someone too soon. People show you who they are sooner or later; usually sooner. It's our job to acknowledge it, and act accordingly."

Upholding Your Values One Tyvek Suit at a Time

Back at the franchise operation from my opening story, things only got worse.

I was sitting at my desk after dispatching my mitigation (MIT) crews for the day. These are the people who show up when you call for assistance after you have experienced water or fire damage in your home or business. We were short staffed, and I was pushing the remaining crews to get out of the shop as soon as possible, attempting to squeeze more hours out of the days.

I was more than a little annoyed when, ten minutes later, two water damage technicians walked up behind my cubicle. "What are you doing here? You are supposed to be on the job site in ten minutes!?"

They expressed that they were sorry but explained, "We

looked through all the vans and couldn't find any Tyvek suits." They were headed to a crawl space job and I had just given them a speech about using proper personal protective equipment (PPE). Here were two employees trying to do things the right way, the way I taught them, but couldn't locate the resources they needed to do so.

"We're completely out of suits? How did that happen?" I asked.

"No," they explained, "We have plenty of suits, upstairs."

"And...?" I asked, starting to get confused.

"You have to get them. We don't have the key," they declared.

My mind was officially blown. Here I was, running a full-service mitigation company for a nationally recognized brand, and my crews didn't have access to the basic tools they needed to effectively do their jobs.

I came to learn why the Tyvek suits, and chem sponges, booties, utility knives and many basic tools of our trade, were under lock and key. In an effort to control costs and maintain inventory logs, a manager had removed all consumables from the warehouse. All of these standard items had to be logged-out and job-costed, according to the rules. A manager (me) and a technician (such as these two who were growing later by the minute) had to initial any materials coming out of the company store room.

I didn't have to run the numbers in order to know that any cost savings and "leakage" prevention as a result of these cumbersome measures would never offset the lost time and productivity involved in maintaining this draconian system. But that wasn't the real cost.

The bigger cost was to the morale of the water damage technicians and the undermining of the culture of the company. Locking everything in the supply closet sent an unambiguous message to the entire company: management doesn't trust you with the most basic of resources, and you have to be "managed" for our company to be successful.

Talk about a buzzkill. My questions to upper management about the impacts of these policies were met with confused looks. I tried to reason with them that we trust our people to enter stranger's houses in the middle of the night, hauling around thousands of dollars of equipment in expensive vans, but we can't trust them with the $5 tyvek suits that they need to safely do their work?

The Impact of our Decisions

As previously mentioned, in his book *The Infinite Game*, Simon Sinek introduces readers to the concept of ethical fading. Ethical fading describes a process whereby a company's culture is slowly eroded to the point where employees begin to make choices which accomplish "corporate" goals at the expense of personal ethics.

A poor culture allows (or does not prevent) employees to make decisions based upon financial gain at the expense of others. Decisions such as opening fake accounts for millions of unsuspecting customers as Wells Fargo did in 2016.

A poor culture enables an organization to increase the price of life saving medicine by 500 fold, as the pharmaceutical company Mylan also did in 2016. While Mylan has not admitted wrongdoing, they are paying a settlement of $465 million[22].

Wells Fargo ended up losing a lot of money as well as a hit to their brand. Their 2016 key performance indicators (KPIs), the number of new accounts signed up in a given month, set the stage for employees having an incentive to open new accounts, regardless of the moral implications. Employees' promotions and bonus structures were heavily weighted on the number accounts opened.

There can be only so many new accounts in any given market. So a creative employee figured out a way to open accounts without a customer's knowledge, and then close them later before the new accounts would show up on bank statements. No harm, no foul, right?

Except when the practice caught on company wide, and bank customers started seeing new accounts show up on their statements. In the end, an estimated 1.5 million checking and savings accounts and over 500,000 credit cards were opened for customers without their authorization.

California Treasurer John Chiang stated:

> "Wells Fargo's fleecing of its customers...demonstrates, at best, a reckless lack of institutional control and, at worst, a culture which actively promotes wanton greed."

> "Blame is being placed on the bank's marketing incentive plan, which set extremely high sales goals for employees to cross-sell additional banking products to existing customers whether or not the customers needed or wanted them."

Wells Fargo's constant drive for an ever increasing share price and greater market share created an environment where dollars and artificial metrics became more important than doing the right thing. Sales targets and growth focused KPIs made sure that the only way to move up the corporate ladder was to push ethical boundaries to the breaking point.

A Forbes article[23] recounts that Wells Fargo admitted to the Department of Justice that they created a culture of, "Unrealistic sales goals that led to thousands of employees opening millions of accounts for customers under false pretenses or without customer consent often by misusing customers' identities." The bank is paying over $3 billion in civil and criminal penalties.

In the absence of strong culture, the only remaining measure of "success" is based on numbers; money. Meeting arbitrary quarterly sales goals, being the "biggest" or "best" in the industry, shaving costs via mass layoffs--these are the things you see from organizations whose only remaining purpose is making and saving money. These companies are playing finite strategies in an Infinite game.

In his previous book, *Leaders Eat Last,* Simon Sinek outlines how the greatest organizations find a way to empower their employees to make the important decisions. Sinek says,

> *"When a leader embraces their responsibility to care for people instead of caring for numbers, then people will follow, solve problems and see to it that that leader's vision comes to life the right way, a stable way and not the expedient way."*

I had to learn the hard way that when you are a leader, you have to follow your gut, especially when it is leading you to do the right thing. As with the example of Joe, if I had addressed the issue when it was small, I may have been able to salvage his tenure with our company. Your culture is built by what you do and each time that you don't act on your ethics, a brick is pulled from the structure.

In *The Innovator's Dilemma,* Clayton Christensen chronicles the repeated failures of companies who were among the most innovative and successful organizations of their times. He describes how companies across sectors, those who achieved market dominance and enviable growth curves, are suddenly and irrevocably overtaken by much more nimble companies.

These new "innovators" seem to come out of nowhere. They quickly move in and completely reinvent whichever market sector they are in. This has been true for steel mills to microchips, the new entrants seemingly out-innovate competitors with budgets and revenues which are orders of magnitude larger.

Christensen observes, "To succeed consistently, good managers need to be skilled not just in choosing, training, and motivating the right people for the right job, but in choosing, building, and preparing the right organization for the job as well." Leaders have to lead by example and in doing so they must work to build a culture that will support and enhance the growth of the company.

When companies rest on their laurels, trusting that what worked yesterday will always work, they are ripe for disruption. While it would seem that innovation is the differentiator, that is not the case. The problem with companies that struggle to remain competitive isn't a lack of ideas, capital, or even motivation. The underlying factors that will aide or undermine the survival of an organization are, "Its resources, its processes, and its values."

CHAPTER 11

A Walk in the Warehouse

By Jon Isaacson

I am sure the reader has at least heard of the popular reality television show Undercover Boss which has been airing on CBS since 2010. Like my family's favorite show, The Office, Undercover Boss was apparently a copy of a British series of the same name. I first became fully aware of the show in 2013 when the company I was working for announced that our CEO would be featured in the program.

My co-workers and I thought *this ought to be good*, being that employees in our property restoration business respond at all hours of the day (or night) to various property damages from water and fire. In this regard the show did not disappoint as our CEO, disguised as his alter ego Tom Kelly, struggled to hang a kitchen cabinet, telling his mentor for the day, "Why don't you come over here and get this up, because this is stupid." We weren't surprised that he broke character, but it was unexpected that he did so after refusing to go into the cleanest crawl space we had ever seen.

The show is popular because it proves what most workers believe, that the suits are disconnected from the everyday workings of their business and even more so, from the everyday people in their organizations. While it is heartwarming when CEO's give generously to the team members that they become acquainted with, I believe the bigger question is how much the experience positively changes the culture of the company.

Long before Undercover Boss popularized the concept of C-suite executives donning terrible wigs and getting some dirt under their fingernails, there were innovative leaders like Ted McCarty who utilized a uniquely effective management practice I like to call, taking a *walk in the warehouse*. You are probably asking, who is this Ted McCarty? We will answer that question but before we do let's take a brief warp back in time. To the years between world wars, and the organization by whom he was called, the iconic guitar manufacturer, Gibson guitars.

On Undercover Boss, it was encouraging to see the CEO of a billion dollar company interact with his people and to learn how dedicated they were to helping their customers recover from disaster. Experiences like this demonstrate that people in a position of leadership are *people* and that they are in a *position* of leadership. In reflecting on his experiences on the show, Sheldon Yellen of BELFOR Property Restoration has remarked,

> "You can't lead with titles, you can't lead with rules, and you can't lead with just words. You lead with trust, compassion, and listening."

As you have observed the value from people in a position of leadership going undercover in their businesses for television, I am excited to share with you the value Ted McCarty derived from being an everyday manager and listening to his employees as he resurrected an icon. Ted exemplifies the principles we are trying to share in this book. I hope the reader will see that small amounts of effort (intentionality), to build a good culture, can result in big returns in your production, and profitability. Whether you are in a rut, or, like Gibson Guitars, on the verge of failure, a few small steps in the right direction can help you make significant progress in your process.

Gibson Guitars in the Pre-McCarty Era

Gibson Guitars, named after its founder Orville Gibson, grew in popularity in the early 1900's as a brand known for its quality acoustic guitars. Perhaps their two most famous instruments are the arched top hollow body acoustic and the Les Paul electric guitar still popular among modern musicians. Yet, you will be surprised to know that the Gibson company had initially taken a hard pass on the opportunity to usher in the dawn of the solid body electric guitar that it is now famous for. If you are a fan of rock and roll, could you imagine Jimmy Page of Led Zepplin or Slash of Guns N' Roses without their Les Pauls?

In 1930, the musician Les Paul[24] brought an ugly little innovation that he called "the log" to the Michigan based manufacturers and they wholeheartedly rejected his innovation. Soon after, an inventor and acquaintance of Paul, who wasn't yet a player in the instrument market, Leo Fender, rose as the first to manufacturer these units in the absence of Gibson's collaboration with Mr. Paul. Even though Leo was first, neither Fender nor Gibson would be strumming for success in this market segment for several years. At the turn of the decade, Gibson wouldn't even be producing instruments at scale as they transformed their factory into a wartime production line.

World War One officially ended in 1918, but things in Europe and abroad were still simmering with tension. Many point to September 1, 1939 when Adolf Hitler's German forces invaded Poland as the final straw that brought the reluctant nations of England and France back into the fray of opposing Nazi expansion. For two years the United States was resolute to avoid participation in the Allied efforts of World War Two. The bombing of Pearl Harbor in Hawaii by the Japanese quickly changed that decision.

> "Yesterday, December 7, 1941 a date which will live in infamy the United States of America was suddenly and deliberately attacked by naval and air forces of the Empire of Japan." - President Franklin D. Roosevelt

A Proud History of Working Women in the Skilled Trades

By early 1942, the United States was in full swing to mount a defense against the advancing threat of a Japanese invasion as well as assisting their Allies to recapture land taken by the Axis forces in Europe. Gibson guitars, like many other manufacturers in the States, transformed their operations into wartime production plants.

At their headquarters in Kalamazoo, Michigan, Gibson hired over 200 women between 1942 to 1946 to make munitions. They came to be known as the Kalamazoo Gals[25] and were responsible for producing upwards of 25,000 of the highly sought after yet secretive Gibson "Banner" guitars.

Necessity gave hard working women an opportunity to display their abilities in the workplace. When the world went to war, even those who were not fighting on the front lines were enlisted to help the military efforts. Our allies in England set the example as, "The British government mobilised civilians more effectively than any other combatant nation. By 1944 a third of the civilian population were engaged in war related work, including over seven million women[26]."

In my industry, property restoration, which is the term we use to describe repairing homes following disasters such as water or fire damage, there have been some great efforts to encourage and celebrate the participation of women in the skilled trades. Michelle Blevins, Editor in Chief for Restoration and Remediation Magazine, started the *Women in Restoration Award* in 2016 to highlight the exceptional efforts of women in this rapidly growing construction segment. All candidates are nominated by their peers and entries are judged based upon the merits of their, "Individual journey, knowledge, and wisdom they had to share, credentials, and so on[27]."

Michelle Blevins joined us for The DYOJO Podcast[28] to discuss the *Ladder Award* to highlight the efforts of industry contributors who are 35 years old and younger (dare we say millennials). People in a position of leadership who are not engaging all candidates in the market are going to struggle to survive. Whether it's workers coming together to help home and business owners recover from disaster or citizens uniting to keep production facilities running, the skilled trades provide opportunities for fulfilling and important work to all sexes, races and ages. As our friends at Kickass Careers so craftily remind us, "Journeyman, it's a status not a gender[29]." Gibson, joined factories across the Allied nations, to produce wood and metal products for the wartime effort in a time of worldwide need.

Resurrecting a Dying Icon

Chicago Musical Instruments (CMI) purchased Gibson Guitars in 1944. As the new owner, Mauric Berlin soon discovered that there was trouble at his headquarters in Kalamazoo. He was sitting at the helm of a company that had an iconic image but was hemorrhaging upwards of $10,000 a month[30] (estimated equivalent to $175,000 in today's dollar). Berlin called upon a former business acquaintance, Ted McCarty, who was an engineer by trade and had been working for the musical manufacturer Wurlitzer for the last 12 years.

McCarty had hit his growth ceiling at Wurlitzer and was ready for a new challenge. Whether Berlin knew it or not, Ted was ready to sign an agreement to become the assistant treasurer with the Brock Candy Company (aka Brach's). Maruric was available for lunch and hungry for talent. By contrast, Brock's decision making ability had stalled when the owner could not be reached while he was on vacation. The Candy Company's delay became the first break for Berlin and the future of his new acquisition at Gibson.

Many organizations lament their struggle to attract and retain good talent while reluctant to adapt their status quo processes. Gibson was quicker to get the pen into the hand of emerging talent than Brock, which brings up a few nuggets for those in a position of leadership to take note of if they want to enhance rather than undermine the growth of their culture:

> Unnecessary bureaucracy will slow your organization down and inhibit your ability to attract good talent.

> Networking is valuable, you never know when your next lunch appointment could lead to a breakthrough.

> If you don't provide ongoing opportunities for your team members they will seek these challenges elsewhere.

Mr. Berlin asked Ted visit Kalamazoo soliciting him to, "Find out what's going on over there, and why I'm losing so much money."[31] Ted took the challenge head on. I think it is interesting to note that Mr. McCarty started his investigation where the action was, he went where the people were who had a direct relationship to the production of the goods. Ted took a *walk in the warehouse.*

When Mr. Yellen was being interviewed for the opening sequence of his episode of Undercover Boss (Season 2, Episode 14), he mentions that the company went through a hiring freeze following the 2008 financial collapse. The company did so in an effort to ensure they could keep as many jobs as possible. He shares some candid thoughts about his employees in 2011; perspectives that many people in a position of leadership share. As he is thumbing through his closet, trying to decide which pair of designer boots to wear for his new blue collar assignment, he comments,

> *"Are there issues that I need to be aware of that do affect the bottom line? Is some equipment not returning back to our shops? Are some of our employees doing side jobs or not?"*

Regardless of your expectations, when those in a position of leadership are willing to join the rank and file in their everyday roles and responsibilities, new perspectives are uncovered. As Dorris Kearns Goodwin says, "Good leadership requires you to surround yourself with people of diverse perspectives who can disagree with you without fear of retaliation." Whether you walk through the warehouse or put on a disguise, when you listen to employees you will gain valuable insights that the other people in suits cannot give you. Mr. Yellen has mentioned in interviews that he encourages his managers to spend at least two days a year in the field with their team members in an effort to continually harvest the benefits of what he learned while on Undercover Boss.

For Ted, walking through the warehouse and initiating real interactions with his team members was a habit. In the span of a week, McCarty was able to observe and glean enough information to acquire a clear picture of what he thought was wrong with the operation at the failing Gibson operation. When the managers on Undercover Boss take a walk through their warehouses, they find that their employees are deeply caring and talented people with vital insights. Ted summed up his findings in a report which likely could be applied to many modern organizations:

> The organization was top heavy.

> The labor force had low morale.

> There were poor employee relations with the current general manager.

> *"We decided that every day we would go through the factory and find one operation that we thought could be improved."* - Ted McCarty on his relationship with John Huis

Fresh Perspectives Uncover Hidden Talent

Ted McCarty was hired by Gibson in 1948, the same year that Leo Fender started producing his *Broadcaster* solid body electric guitar. Upon arrival in Kalamazoo, Ted's first visit was back to the production floor where many of the issues revolved around poor management from then general manager Guy Hart. If morale continued in its low state, the transformation Ted was orchestrating would be undermined by the lack of harmony between employees and management.

Ted's walks in the warehouse allowed him to identify an employee who had been overlooked for 15 years, John Huis. Their partnership expanded his understanding of the problems while also helping Ted to identify solutions. When promotion is conducted without alignment to vision and values, poor management mindset and habits undermine progress, production, and profitability. Getting the right people in the right seats (as outlined in *Good To Great* by Jim Collins) requires the courage to STOP promoting based on convenience and START aligning roles and responsibilities with vision and values.

I am so grateful that many of my managers saw something in me that I didn't always see in myself. Sharon taught me in that small drive-thru in Moses Lake, Washington that the size of your operation doesn't matter when developing a clear and consistent process leading to excellence. She didn't care about the age of her employees when empowering them to rise to her expectations and hold the team accountable for the established standards. If Sharon was still with us and I went back to ask her questions about her "leadership" she would probably laugh in my face after she slapped it. She was not a fan of jargon, she was a doer. If you read this book but don't apply anything to your roles, responsibilities, and organizations, Sharon would gladly slap you as well.

When I was working with Denis, I did not want to be in management, I thought my career path was leading me into criminal justice. What I learned, which is a challenge I have given to many people since, is that if I didn't step up someone else was going to. It took one bad manager[32] for me to realize that the wrong mindset and habits in a position of leadership would negatively impact my team members and the progress that we had built. Managers must defend their culture from threats foreign (external) and domestic (internal).

We had a good team, the kind of team that makes even a poorly performing manager look good. Too many that come in as "leaders" or "superstars" don't take the time to learn the strengths and weaknesses of the team before they launch into their pre-set programs. I have learned time and time again that the core values of what I believe lead to success remain the same but the applications are different with each assignment. The organizations are unique, as are the markets and the team members.

In following through on his list of key corrections, Ted believed that there were too many foremen resulting in glaring inconsistencies in production. There needed to be a central superintendent who was responsible for oversight of all the sections. McCarty promoted Huis to this new key role and Hart resigned. The hidden gem (Huis) was promoted and the cancer (Huis) was removed. Empowering John to improve the production systems enabled Ted to move on to bigger issues within the organization, as they worked together to enhance the new culture at Gibson.

I believe the moment when my career path in property restoration took an upward trajectory was simultaneous with the moment when I was ready to walk away. I preach clarity because I believe in it. A lack of clarity is incredibly frustrating. On this particular day, we had met as a team in our huddle and received our assignments. I knew what I was supposed to be doing and felt I was clear on the scope of work as well as the target duration. When our assistant manager stopped by the job, I was instructed to change my course and work in a different area. I respectfully questioned the new direction but acquiesced as this person often was temperamental and vindictive.

I think this is important to note, as a person in a position of leadership, especially if you are an owner, you need to ensure that your management representatives understand the vision and are executing their duties in relationship to those values. There often is a disconnect between what a company says and what a company does at the management level which undermines credibility and progress. Do you hire, develop, and hold those in positions of leadership in your organization accountable to the process?

When my manager, Denis, stopped by, he asked why I was working in the area. I was frustrated. I had my assignment that morning. I thought I was clear on what I should be doing and where I was going to start. Midway through the morning our assistant manager had changed it and now shortly after lunch our manager was changing it again; or at least questioning it for the second time. I remember saying something to the effect of, "You guys need to get your stories straight, I am getting really frustrated with the feeling that I am doing it wrong when I am doing what you said."

Denis built access and communication into his system, we started each day in the office reviewing our progress from the day prior as well as our assignment for the current day. Because Denis was good about visiting multiple job sites throughout the week, we had regular access to him throughout the workday. He listened and thankfully when I shared my frustration a change was made in management. This conversation was the last straw in the process and Denis realized there was a growing dissonance between the culture he was trying to build and the undermining effects of a person who did not operate in alignment with the vision and values.

It may not sound like a big deal, but those instances of assignments changing not based upon new information or need but because someone in "power" was not operating with clarity, consistency, or accountability brought my frustration to a boil.

In the current market, jobs aren't that hard to come by, in many ways your organization needs its people more than the people need your organization. If you want to attract, develop, and retain good talent, it's important to identify and stop undermining your culture.

> *"We were growing, from 150 employees, growing and growing and growing, and we had about 1,200 when I left in '66."* Ted McCarty on growth

The Positive Effects of Empowering People

Not only did Ted listen to employees, he shockingly believed that being friendly with the staff was important. He even went so far to make it his goal, with *only* 150 employees, to remember the names of individuals as well as something significant about them as people. This commitment, in combination with acting on his observations from above, transformed the attitude of the employees towards management. McCarty and Huis continued to collaborate and decided to walk the warehouse floor daily to find an operation that they thought could be improved. Ted understood the impact of leading by example, to hold himself and his core leaders accountable for the change in culture, as well as the commitment to growth.

By identifying issues, taking action, and empowering people, McCarty and Gibson went from bleeding money in March to making a profit by May of 1949. Ted was Vice President within a year and President of Gibson by 1950. Revamping the culture was critical to restoring a dying brand. Ted had clarity, consistency, and accountability working in the organization. He was enjoying his work, employees were thriving in a positive environment, and the organization was firing on all cylinders.

When I would visit offices for local agents and prospective clients following Undercover Boss, the reviews were mixed. Our company already had a target on our back as one of the largest organizations in our industry. Some people fixed on our CEO's wardrobe, the size of the company, and his efforts to build a golf course as reasons to believe that we were "too big" to be local. Some clients appreciated how relatable he appeared to be as demonstrated by how often he cried during his interactions with everyday employees.

One thing that I could confidently say to detractors, or those on the fence, was that his interaction with Jen led to her becoming involved with training at the corporate level. Sheldon found a hidden gem and promoted her to a role that seemed to be more fulfilling for her and became a point of encouragement for many. One of my team members attended a training course that she taught and from what I can see on LinkedIn she is still with the company.

Something as high profile as Undercover Boss proves that you can never please everyone. The show maintains high viewer ratings but feedback for each CEO varies. As a person in a position of leadership, no one will ever fully understand what you are doing and why, but it is to your benefit to communicate your vision as clearly as you are able. Your commitment to your values is tested by your ability to remove those practices (or people) who *undermine* your progress as well as making decisions that *enhance* the culture you are working to develop. The process is never complete, it's an everyday effort.

> *"I was working with the rest of the engineers, and we would sit down, like in a think tank, and we would talk about this guitar: Let's do this, let's try that."* - Ted McCarty on innovating with his team

A Strong Culture, Endless Opportunities

With Gibson back in the business of making guitars it was now time to improve the position of the business in their market. They weren't the first to market for the solid body electric guitar but Ted was instrumental (pun intended) in building an innovative culture. They started by brokering a napkin deal with

Les Paul to be the public face of their electric guitar which bore his name and launched in 1952.

Ted McCarty was never a musician and yet he had a 60 plus year career with three successful companies in the industry. He is regarded as a key figure in "the golden years of Gibson", having a hand in many of the features that brought about the evolution of the solid body electric guitar. How was Ted able to leave such a mark in the industry? When he wanted to fix the factory, he listened to the employees. So, he took the same approach to revolutionizing the guitar - listen to guitar players. His team focused on quality and made adaptations that addressed the needs of musicians.

The reader will recall that Gibson had taken a hard-pass on the guitar innovation back in the 1930's. Yet, even after Fender brought his unit to the market there were many manufacturers who still thought it was just a fad. Ted was undeterred when his competitors told him, "Anyone with a bandsaw can make a solid body guitar. Bandsaw and a router, that's all you need." Ted sought ways to innovate without sacrificing the quality that had built their company's brand.

> *"Fender was talking about how Gibson was a bunch of old fuddie-duddies...I was a little peeved. So I said, 'Let's shake 'em up.' I wanted to come up with some guitar shapes that were different from anything else."* - Ted McCarty on maintaining a competitive edge

Sharpen Your Skills Together

Ted left splashes of his fiercely competitive nature. One of the signature features of the initial Gibson Les Paul was the arched top which Ted incorporated primarily because he wanted, "To do something Leo Fender couldn't do." When rival Fender called Gibson out for it's archaic approaches to the market, McCarty made it his personal mission to launch designs that had never been seen. The Flying V, Explorer, and Moderne came out of this competitive drive, which weren't commercially successful at the time but have experienced periods of popularity in more recent years.

McCarty developed key collaborations from within, and without, to the benefit of Gibson. He also was able to guide the successful acquisition and integration of their competitor Epiphone to drive his vision of expanding their capacity to compete in the market for bass guitars. McCarty led Gibson from hemorrhaging money to consistent profitability which steadily increased 15 times. His sales grew by 1,250 percent, the work force expanded tenfold and production went from 5,000 to 100,000 guitars per annum.

It seems it is impossible to grow as an organization without accumulating your share of detractors. BELFOR has an impressive history of acquisitions which have contributed to its immense growth as a consistent industry leader. Mr. Yellen and his team have an eye for opportunity. Sheldon noted retrospectively about his time on Undercover Boss, "There should be a golden rule of sorts when it comes to running a business and delegating duties. The greatest leaders are willing to roll up their sleeves and complete whatever tasks they typically assign to frontline workers. They must be able and willing to do whatever it is they ask their team members to do."[33]

> *"I went there [to Gibson] on March 15, we lost money in March, we lost money in April, we made money in May, and we made it for the next 18 years—never had a loss. I left there in '66, when I bought this company from Paul Bigsby."* - **Ted McCarty** on his achievements at Gibson

Sustainability Doesn't Require Complexity

McCarty continued his habit of walking the warehouse floor at Gibson where he could see the issues clearly and hear directly from his team members. In later years, McCarty saw that trouble with leadership was on the horizon and he decided to look for opportunities elsewhere. Good talent can slip through your organization's fingers in many forms including:

Slow hiring processes

Poor engagement

Overlooking internal talent

Devaluing contributors

Ted, and then Vice President John Huis, resigned at Gibson in 1966. Together they started a new venture as owners of Bigsby Accessories, Inc. While the partnership between Gibson and McCarty did not endure the test of time, his relationship with that hidden gem John Huis did. By the time they left Gibson Guitars, McCarty had direct involvement, if not primary influence, in such innovations as the Tune-o-matic bridge system, the humbucking pickup, and the Flying V guitar, to name a few.

It should be no surprise that McCarty at 56 years old still had fuel in the tank and was successful at Bigsby, implementing many of the same core values and cultural distinctives in the new company. The power duo of Ted McCarty and John Huis understood the importance of enhancing, and not undermining, their culture. In a humorous twist of fate, Bigsby was purchased from McCarty in 1999 by Gretsch who then sold the company in 2019 to none other than Ted's rival Fender.

In property restoration, there are many growth minded professionals who donate their time, knowledge, and experiences to assist their industry fellows in raising the bar. I have heard more than one community member echo the sentiment that "rising tides raise all ships" including one of the first mentions of it on The DYOJO Podcast[34] with Whatley. We started a podcast within the podcast, something we call Pro vs. Joe, which has helped me to remember not to take my experiences for granted. While it often isn't intentional, those who have been in an industry for an extended period of time, can forget what it was like to be at the entry level again. Connecting with ground floor employees, new entrepreneurs, and growth minded young people can help reinvigorate your passion for your craft.

In later years, McCarty was brought out of retirement by Paul Reed Smith who credits Ted as being a key mentor to his own success. Ted was legally blind by the time they met in the 80's but his ideas were still clear. Paul said that he became aware of McCarty when he visited the U.S. patent office and noticed that Ted's name was attributed to so many of Gibson's key innovations. As we said, while you may have never heard about Ted McCarty, there is much to learn from his story that can be applied to any organization. Enhancing your culture doesn't have to be complex. The process starts with something as simple as removing those status quo mindset and habits that undermine your efforts.

Unfortunately, Ted is no longer with us but there are many takeaways that you can glean from the methods of Mr. McCarty in transforming an organization from dysfunctional and under-performing (even moribund) to a competitive force in the market.

Six Culture Enhancing Habits from Ted McCarty's Managerial Playbook:

> When in doubt, take a walk in the warehouse. Conduct your own regular runs as an Undercover Boss by rolling up your sleeves and mixing it up with your team members on the front lines.

> Be a *person* in a position of leadership. You are a human working with humans. Being friendly, talking with and listening to employees, can produce valuable interactions with your team and unearth key insights that would be missed without these habits.

> *"In my opinion, being an effective leader requires being an effective listener. Success is more often attained by asking 'how?' than by saying 'no.'"* - Coach John Wooden

> Pull the trigger on talent. Keep your eyes open so that you can identify your key assets, some of whom may currently

be overlooked and undervalued, as well as your core detractors, some of whom may currently be overvalued and have too much influence.

Keep your processes nimble. Unnecessary bureaucracy will weigh you down. Be ready to act upon what you discover and follow through with what you say. Management and processes should serve the people while executing the process.

Disrupt yourself. How can you expect your team or your organization to adapt and innovate if you don't? Be intentional with your habits by challenging yourself to change and grow as a person in a position of leadership.

"Learning and innovation go hand in hand. The arrogance of success is to think that what you did yesterday will be sufficient for tomorrow." - William Pollard

Lead by Example. Keep your mind engaged by finding things that interest you in your business. Be competitive and empower others to fill in with their areas of strength. Pursue those things that hill enhance the culture you are seeking to build while having the courage to stop doing those things that undermine your culture.

CHAPTER 12

Shifting Lives: Yesterday,
Today, and Tomorrow

By David Princeton

Yesterday

Death. Shifts. Everything.

Forty minutes from home, talking about claims in a client's conference room. That all too familiar vibration. Ignore. Vibration again, this time a call. Ignore. Vibration again, another call. Excused myself, out in the hall. Everything. Shifted. Forever--Death.

Death. Five long years ago that moment set about a change, eventually leading me to find a new perspective on life and tomorrow.

Life. Terry, my father-in-law, always bet on himself in any situation, even when the odds seemed stacked against him. A serial entrepreneur, who had success in the late 70's early 80's doing advertising and marketing before computers. Bankruptcy and a few other failed business attempts, he never quit trying, no matter the odds, his last attempt was a jalapeno dried spice that could light up the blandest of meals!

Doing. I did not know what I was seeing when he was here.

For 15 years I witnessed Terry come up with an idea, take to doing the work, and despite set-backs still looked for ways to grind. Displaying courage in the face of adversity. I was risk averse, always full of ideas, but never acted. I was a grinder, no doubts, but I was scared to bet on myself. I was content to take the safety of a paycheck. I did what a lot of people do--come in early, leave late, serve the interest of my employer. I had a good job, supporting others in their interests, being relied on and a go-to person in difficult situations. I got incredible results, often doing what others deemed impossible.

Shift. Four months after losing Terry, my wife is still unable to function, an opportunity presented. A top executive that I wanted to meet with and talk about my future. I had no idea what to expect. The day before our meeting I made it a point to work from the HQ, just in the off chance I would run into the executive. The office is about ninety minutes from home. I arrive before the sun, and I start my day. 5 o'clock comes and goes... my day is not done. It was about Seven o'clock and I put a bow on it. As I am walking towards the stairs, that chance encounter happens.

Standing at his desk, looking over a few web platforms, we get to chatting. He flip's his screen around and shows me a law school's webpage. "Why aren't you here?" In a heartbeat, seven excuses spewed forth, without thinking. What just happened?

The drive home, stone silence.

Thoughts racing faster than I'm driving.

The return trip the next morning, more time to think.

As a child, I would often challenge points being made, or see a different meaning or angle in words and situations. Often enjoying the technicalities of games, situations, rules, and also sticking up for others that couldn't stick up for themselves. When I graduated with my bachelors degree, I had taken the entrance exam but did not pursue Law School further. I was lucky to land a job in the crisis of the time, and excited to start working. I took this piece of me, this part of my soul, and I put it on a shelf. As time passed, I convinced myself that I would go to law school after I retired, when I had the time, and did not need to sacrifice.

The next morning, we met. I resolved that I would get out of my own way and pursue law school, and the company would help me in that pursuit. I could not believe what I was hearing... Now all I have to do is—get into law school!

The Executive saw through me. He saw that I was not living up to my potential. I had more to give this world and all it took was someone to get me out of my own way, and for me to learn from Terry—Always be willing to bet on yourself, if you're not —no one else will!

Getting into Law School is not easy...at least not for me. The application process is lengthy. The entrance exam is not for the timid. The first year I applied, I was late in the cycle. Applications already started being filed months before I would take the December entrance exam. How hard can this be? After all, I had a month to prepare.

My score... not great.

My GPA...not stellar.

My application... waitlist.

My desire—fully fueled.

My second year applying. 4am - 7:30am 5 days a week studying before work. This goes on for months. Two more exams taken. My score...not better than the first time. Amazing letters of recommendation—clients, company leaders, and attorneys all professing "he's worthy" of the education.

My application...waitlist.

My desire—unwavering!

Fortitude. My third year applying. Private tutor, 5pm-10pm 5 days a week. Saturday and Sunday 8 hours a day. January – June. Literally, I took every LSAT ever released. Analyzed my performance, reviewed with the tutor. My personal best in practice was a 160. I take the official test, 155. I prepare my application materials, and in the first few minutes that applications were accepted I applied. September, 2018, three years after that meeting with the Exec.

My desire—starting to waiver.

Life. A few weeks after applying, my wife's job was eliminated, the last few years we had more than our fair share of struggles. Through it all, we've learned to go with the flow. You only get disappointed if you deviate from the path, but as long as you arrive at the destination—enjoy the journey. I start to doubt that all the time, energy, money, and work will result in making my dream a reality.

Will I finally get accepted to law school or will this be just another waitlist letter?
It was early-October, 2018 I get a call. A different company wanted to talk about my future. An offer of a lifetime? I decided to accept the offer. Life was moving fast. I made the trip to the HQ, I thought it was right that the Exec. would be the first to know of the departure. We talked briefly, he was happy for me.

Shifting lives.

My last day was at the end of October, 2018. On November 3, 2018 my wife and I are picking up a new car. We get an email from USPS, letting us know what is arriving in the mail that day. We had signed up for daily digital scans of our mail a few years ago, after rushing home on countless lunch breaks to look for a letter from Law School. I checked the scan and a letter from Law School. Not a big envelope, like in the movies, but I noticed that the letter was from the Dean and not the admission's department. Good news?

I descend upon the mailbox, clawing for the letter. Carefully opening the edge. "Congratulations, we wish to inform you. . .." I got in! My first call was to the Exec. of the company I just left a few days ago after 5+ years of being a part of something special. He takes my call, on a Saturday. We talk. I hang-up and tears come to my eyes. August, 2019 I would start Law School, part-time, 4 years after the conversation that got me motivated to live for my dreams. Hanging on the walls at home, nicely framed, the waitlist letters. A reminder of what can be accomplished with a lot of work and persistence.

Today

Collapse? Birth! Fate.

July, 2019. The company I am working for is on the brink of collapse. Complicated insurance claims, cash flow issues, regulatory authorities conducting investigations, and partners who don't want to be partners. Divesting isn't easy, especially with 120 families depending on a job.

Birth! I take a deep breath, birthing a limited liability corporation focused on helping businesses navigate complex claims. My passion, even before, was making the seemingly impossible, plausible or better yet, occur. I am not afraid to bet on my-self anymore. I know nothing is going to keep me from pursuing my legal education. I start to spend a few hours a week building a website, forming a game plan, working on making something from nothing.

Law School starts, it is amazing! I have longed to be challenged since graduating college and to be back, learning. My soul is alive! I was still working full-time, helping a company survive.

I was staying up late, doing school-work. Then my business gets a call. Then another call. Then I am retained as an insurance claim practices expert in a lawsuit. I have several of my own clients, the demands of my day job, and law school. Sleep became a luxury, but I was happy. I was leaning into my talents. I was making a difference in the lives of my clients, helping a company continue to survive, and for the first time in a long time—felt purposeful.

Fate. Something in the universe is making November important. My wife, her bestie, and the husbands attend a masquerade ball, as part of an image relaunch of a fancy hotel. It was an evening filled with artistic performances, a witty poet, and, for me, a chance to pay forward. Making our way around the event I see a familiar face stroll through the door, Patrick. A younger man, with swagger that can light up a room. He had graduated college a few years prior and we worked together for a while, as he went through a career development program. To meet this guy, you know he is wired to be in business development. Patrick has a god given talent to engage in easy conversation that feels meaningful, and to leave someone better than how he found them.

Surprise washes over me as Patrick tells me his story. He is not doing business development. Instead he chose a different path. He is an Account Executive. Once viewed as the career path he wanted most, he is now focused on only a few clients, looking to grow an organic book of business, and I can see he is not happy. We talk. REALLY TALK! He was looking for something, but could not figure out what. He had some feelers out, but nothing was feeling like a good fit. Shifting lives. After twenty minutes we figured out that his ego got in the way when he chose to be an Account Executive. Just as I described him, he has been told how he is naturally wired for business development. Rather than embrace his gifts and turn pro, he felt a need to prove he could do something else. Perhaps he felt like others were saying he couldn't —be an amazing Account Executive.

Been there, done that. Here was Patrick, wanting to do what I had already done, wanting to make a change for the wrong reasons. About to make the mistakes that I've already made. Patrick had a choice, either find a different place to do a job that does not make him happy, or he could have the difficult conversation and own his mistake. No matter what happens, he needed to lean into his talents and own his natural abilities, focusing instead on becoming vs proving others wrong. I left Patrick with a warning, "if he starts running now, he will be running his entire career."

A few months later, I received a text. Patrick wants to connect. We met. He had a difficult conversation. He owned his mistake of choosing the Account Executive track instead of going into a Business Development role. Patrick was leaving the company, with no opportunity lined up, and he has never been happier! Patrick told me about how he was gaining weight, stressed out, and just not enjoying what he was doing. He loved where he worked, loved the professionals he got to team with, but it just was not a role that he found fulfilling. Despite having to figure out a departure plan, he was excited about the future. For the first time in a while he was back to embracing who he is, fundamentally! Shifting lives. Just as Patrick's time at the company was coming to a close a new opportunity presented itself. It was a business development role with a different company in the same industry.

Fortunately, Patrick made the right choice. He had the difficult conversation. He admitted that being an Account Executive was a mistake for him. He talked about how he is denying part of himself that longs to bring together people with effective solutions and creating a story that speaks impactfully to the issues faced by a prospective client. Patrick likes to solve problems, and find the next problem to solve.

Tomorrow

Mistakes. Experience. Shift.

2015 an Exec. got me out of my own way, and I messed up that relationship in 2018 by how I left. I should have had the difficult conversation. I should have shared my life, challenges, and aspirations. In 2019, I saw someone about to make the same mistake. The difference for Patrick, was the benefit of sharing an experience, regrets, and mistakes. Patrick's life shifted. My life shifted. All because someone took the time to challenge self-imposed limitations.

The worst thing that can happen is the passing of time. Tomorrow is promised to no one. My awakening was the loss of Terry. It took a push to get me off the bench and into the game of pursuing what is wired into me, fundamentally! How many moments have passed in which you are denying who you are, fundamentally? Each of those moments can never be taken back, but you decide what the next moment looks like. You get to embrace the next moment, get off the bench and start doing. The most important part is the doing.

Mistakes. Along the way I will make mistakes. Lots of mistakes. But that is one of the beautiful things about life, learning from those mistakes. I now make it a point to share my mistakes with others, hoping that expressing a vulnerability will empower them to make a better decision than I made. Everyone's experience is uniquely their own and sharing that experience can lead to some incredible things!

Experience. While I am still trying to help a company survive, still trying to get my own company off the ground, and still going to Law School, I don't waste time by putting obstacles in my own way. Time is the most important thing we have, I choose to spend it with the people who won't replace me, doing the things that make me happy! Surround yourself with people who view you as essential. If your presence did not matter to them when you were there, it won't matter when you are gone.

Shift. The ripple that can be created when you start to lean into who you are can be an incredible feeling. Patrick and I are now developing a podcast, looking to bring together people who want to do, are doing, and have done, _<fill-in-the-blank>_. It's about the power of sharing experience, at a human level across people's desires and ambitions. If you want to do, are doing, or have done something – let's connect and see how the power of experience can shift lives!

CHAPTER 13

Priming The Pump On Culture

By Chris Stanley

Toxic vibes and members penetrate nearly every group on Facebook, forums, LinkedIn, and anywhere else people gather on the internet. Negative Nancy's and Debbie Downers tend to be the main people that have anything to say. When someone goes looking for answers from human beings about how to do something, they are often met with fierce resistance and combative responses.

This type of culture poisons passion, ruins relationships, and often derails any change that a person was attempting to make in their life. The internet makes everyone faceless and the bullies are bigger and badder than any school playground bully could ever attempt to be. Often times these individuals don't even know they are bullies, they think they are just telling people "That is how it is."

That is unless the groups have a culture of giving, caring, and looking to genuinely help each other. As I set about creating my own niche online group, I set out to do one thing, to make it a safe place to ask questions.

I wasn't sure how to achieve that. Would I have to be a tyrant kicking everyone out who strayed from the way things were done? That sounds like the opposite of the culture I wanted. I didn't have the answers, so I did the only thing I knew how to do... answer questions.

As more and more people came into our paid community, we encouraged them that "No question was a dumb question." We informed them that "We've all been there and want to help."

The result, people started asking questions... lots of questions.

The first wave of people that joined got long-winded answers full of everything I could think to tell them about the topic. If I couldn't type everything I wanted to say I'd point to websites, videos, or other resources that would give them their answer. I'd spend hours answering question after question. It was exhausting and as we added more members I was scared I wouldn't be able to keep up the pace. I worried I'd burn out and the culture would be ruined. If I didn't answer their questions... who would? I needed a break.

I chose an impromptu 3-day weekend and announced to my community that I'd be absent, but I'd be back on Tuesday. I disconnected and prayed I'd still have a community to talk to when I returned. I'd promised myself I wouldn't look at the community for three days, but I fretted much of the long weekend. These people had paid me money for answers and I just ditched them.

I powered on my computer on Tuesday and scrolled through to see tons of questions. I took a deep breath and swallowed hard, prepared to dive in giving answers. Then I noticed something. All of the questions had been answered by other community members. They were helping each other. Many of their answers were better and more relevant than what I would have offered.

I jumped in and made comments like, "I totally agree with @John Smith. That is good advice." or offered my own advice and opinion on ones I felt hadn't quite been answered properly.

This community didn't stop answering each other's questions that Tuesday, they kept on doing it. Soon I barely had to answer questions, ever! I became a cheerleader in a community and in over 2 years and 400+ community members I've never had to kick someone out for being rude.

I get comments frequently mentioning how our community is so different from all those other groups. The dream of having a safe place to ask questions had been realized.

Often, we as leaders feel that the people we serve and work with just don't have the same culture as we do. They lack the work ethic, don't

think like we do, or revert to bad habits the
moment we move our attention away from managing them.

Although I can take no genius from my accidental success, I can take lessons from it. Culture cannot be created from a vacuum. The people who you bring together as a group will not
automatically have the same culture as you do. There are as many different cultures as there are people, but you need to start by setting the pace.

Like leading a group of racers you need to show them how you are racing, how you are working, how you deal with situations. You start off by leading. You are the one to prime the pump of culture, but it isn't a sustainable pace. At some point you must step back and let someone else lead. You may have to take a break or even appoint someone else as "lead of the community" and see if the culture holds without you at the front. Good culture lasts even when you aren't
present.

You'll need to check back in on your various groups and cheerlead their efforts, tweak their responses, run with them a mile, then let them continue on without you. You can't be the
culture, but you must start by living the culture publicly for all to see. You'll have to give everything you've got to that culture and then turn it loose to see if it lives on without you.

If it does you've got something that will last, something special. You'll have a group of people that not only will follow your lead, but lead in your absence.

On a practical level, there are things you can do to help eliminate un-necessary questions as a leader. Part of being a good leader is providing the answers and support for the tasks you know that the people you lead will face.

No leader enjoys answering the same questions over and over again, so it is to our advantage to realize the questions that are being asked (or should be being asked) and to deliver answers and solutions.

What I've found when training and supporting my community is that there is a way to answer 90% of the questions before they ever ask them. This makes the questions that do get asked richer and builds up those in the community with specific situations and not just the same things over and over again. I use a 3 part structure to provide answers to these common questions. The structure I use to tackle the common questions is framework, cheat guides, and videos.

Before you roll your eyes, say it isn't applicable to your business, and tune out, ask yourself this question. What if as a leader you could eliminate 90% of all the questions you get asked over and over again and could simply offer your expertise and advice on the uniqueness of a situation? What would that do for you, for your team, your business, and your culture? Let's look at this structure that you can build to support your people.

Framework

Often people don't even know what questions to ask so they can never discover the answers themselves. It isn't that people are stupid, they just don't know... what they don't know. The main reason for the framework is so those you lead know which questions to ask themselves. By building a decision making framework for the group they have a process by which they can find the answers on their own.

The framework I use asks 7 questions and is easy to remember and visual in nature. It provides a common way to process the problems we face so even when questions are asked we are all looking at it the same way. This can also simply be a workflow chart or a list of to-do's for a given step of a project. Don't make it complicated, the goal is to make it simple.

Fast food restaurants have a system by which to build a sandwich, aka a framework. Choose your bread, slap the mayo on, then the burger, etc. The questions they then begin to ask are things like, "What type of bread should this sandwich have? Does it get mayo?"

This is the type of framework by which you are looking to build, one that prompts the correct questions.

Cheat Guides

Nearly every industry does things the same way over and over again. There are spoken and unspoken rules that you must abide by. These can be legal, safety, or just common sense rules that keep you and your team on the straight and narrow. The problem is we can't assume our people know or remember what they are.

Once someone is asking the right questions using a framework, the cheat guide provides the answer to the question. Creating this can be the most time intensive part of building this support structure. It may be frustrating to try and figure out how to create cheat guides for what seems like to you, the obvious answer, but this can save you hours a day plus make your team more efficient.

There is a reason big companies have scripts (aka cheat guides) for customer service calls. There is a reason McDonalds makes a hamburger the same way every time and has it posted where those creating the sandwiches can see it. These cheat guides answer the question as soon as they know what to ask.

Video

You've given your team a decision making framework that makes them ask the right questions, is this a sesame seed bun or Texas Toast for this sandwich? Then you provided them with a cheat guide that answers the question they knew to ask with a cheat guide. Oh yeah the Big Mac needs the sesame seed bun. The last and truly transformative part for you the leader is to provide videos of how to now execute what they know they must do.

Video is so easy to do these days and you don't need to worry about quality. Turn on your cell phone and go selfie style. Did someone ask you the right way to install a plug on your construction crew? Record yourself installing on. Take time and answer the question once and save the video. Put it to a page on your website, create your own private YouTube Channel, and build a list of common questions with links to the answers.

Need to show someone how to do something on the computer? There are tons of free software that allows you to screen record. Show your team once how to do it and record the session. You've now answered a common how-to question that will come up ONCE. When someone asks that question in the future you'll be able to direct them to where to find the answer.

This is how you not only maintain your culture, but maintain and grow your business. By empowering your people and not babysitting them, you are able to do the things a leader should be doing and not be someone who has to sit and answer the same questions day after day.

CHAPTER 14

A Leadership Fable: Listen

By Jon Isaacson

There once was a business leader
You may know him rather well
He knew that change was coming
But how to get there he could not tell
So he paced and he pranced
As thoughts in his leadership mind danced

Daily he scurried about
Going to and fro
But never did he pause to listen
If answers from within he could glisten
He made a call from without
And decided to spend a great deal of money
Still never pausing to see
If his own hive had any honey

When the dollars were spent
And nothing had changed
He turned to his team members
But they were estranged
The ship had long sailed

As the leader refused to listen
Let this short story serve as your warning lesson

Orl you too may find
All those who would will not any more

If you really want to rock the dial on the cringe-o-meter, I created a video for this little diddy several years ago. You can't get the full experience without watching and listening to medicore prose on the unremarkable DYOJO YouTube.

PART 3:

Small Things, Big Impacts

CHAPTER 15

*Helping Yourself So That
You Can Help Others*

By Jon Isaacson

Identity, honesty, and adaptability are key to growing as a professional as well as an organization. Having a clear sense of identity is important for leaders and organizations. Clarity is key to culture as a lack of clarity undermines any effort to build it. In the play Hamlet, William Shakespeare speaking through Polonius provides this fatherly advice,

> *"This above all: to thine own self be true,
> and it must follow, as the night the day,
> thou canst not then be false to any man."*

A clear identity enables people in a position of leadership and teams to be honest with each other as they seek to compete in business. Honesty among individuals, as well as within teams, facilitates real time adaptability to changes in the market that are critical to sustained success. Let's break down the quote from Polonius to peel through the layers that will enhance our growth mindset as people seeking to develop strong cultures.

Developing Your Identity as a Person in a Position of Leadership

A clear identity enables leaders and teams to be honest with each other as they seek to compete in business. Honesty among individuals, as well as within teams, facilitates real time adaptability to changes in the market that are critical to sustained success. Only a person in a position of leadership who understands themselves can help to define and build a culture that will empower others to do the same.

"This above all else..."

You must prioritize. There's isn't enough time, money or resources to do everything. There are limits and they can demotivate you or force you to take the smartest risks you can imagine. To activate your growth mindset you cannot lose touch with reality. You must learn the ever evolving terrain, rules, resources, and limitations of the modern workplace. Reality is not the enemy, it is essential to growth.

Where are we now (brutal honesty)

Where are we headed (what is our potential)

What must we do to reach our goals (or at least fight valiantly to compete)

Author of Organizational Physics, Lex Sisney, has composed **Three Covenants** of operating agreements to help teams maximize input and buy in. Covenant 3 states, "The goal is frank and honest discussion of the facts before a decision is made, followed by total commitment to implementing the solution after the decision is made."[35]

Those in a position of leadership do well to understand that they need as broad a net of inputs as possible from within as well as without their team. As we learned in my previous chapter with Ted McCarty, when a leader listens, they open themselves to valuable input. Failure to listen to those who are in the field distributing your products or services, those front line employees, is cutting your organization off from valuable perspectives.

Managers must also understand that **conflict** is not by its own nature a negative thing. Creating an open and honest culture where ideas flow without filters requires space for dissension among equals. A team can create healthy boundaries for discussion by remaining civil as they disagree. while making clear the timeline for disagreement and the expectation of buy in once the decision is made. As Sisney put it, "Put another way, it's OK to question a decision up front but it's not OK to fight it or ignore it during implementation."

A leader who is confident in their strengths is able to create opportunities for employees to exercise theirs.

"To thine own self…"

Organizations that struggle with their identity will struggle to clarify their value proposition in the marketplace. Organizational culture and identity sound like such lofty concepts but they are merely reflections of the teams day to day actions and the identity of the leadership. Your company culture is what you do. Your organizational identity often mirrors that of your leadership. We make culture and identity abstract when we try to create them rather than recognize what they are and then optimize them.

Three questions for increasing employee engagement towards achieving team goals:

Do you understand who you are as an individual?

> Regardless of your rung on the corporate ladder, knowing who you are is valuable to your personal and professional growth as well as to your ability to help your team.

> What are your strengths and weaknesses?

Do you understand who you are as a team?
> Whether you are a niche group that handles one aspect of a much larger entity or a broad based group that covers a large list of responsibilities, can you articulate your culture?

> Would individual team members reach consensus on their collective roles, responsibilities and values?

Do you understand who you are as an organization?

> Regardless of the size of your company, do you know your place in the market and have you clarified your value proposition?

> Does your team know your company story and are they inspired to share that good news through their work and public interactions?

Leadership starts with holding yourself accountable

In **The Real Life MBA,** Jack and Suzy Welch write, "The only reason to talk about behaviors at work is that leaders need to be very public, very clear, and very consistent about what kind of behaviors are needed in order to achieve the company's mission." Leaders must lead by example, it should be the working definition of leadership but often it falls short of action.

When those in a position of leadership understand themselves they free up capacity to find and build other leaders who will round out the team needs so that the mission can move forward. When leaders don't understand themselves they often lead by fear and hold the team back from reaching its potential.

> Clarity comes from truth.

> Collaboration comes from a willingness to receive input.

By combining clarity with collaboration, leaders, teams, and organizations will unlock the capacity to compete. The funny thing about teamwork is that it is not created or fixed by teamwork. When you have a lack of teamwork the answer is not add more teamwork. If we had three people in a boat and told them to row hard, would this get us where we want to go? The answer is no because we have not defined where we are going nor have we clarified how we are going to work together to get there. Too often dysfunction is not a symptom of a lack of effort but a lack of clarity. Three rowers giving a hundred percent but not rowing in the same direction or in harmony will result in a boat that is rapidly spinning in circles.

When it comes to deficiencies in teamwork, inexperienced leaders will address unity as its own source when in reality it is a symptom. If by now, you still think that culture magically appears because you talk about unity, downloaded a training on cooperation, or have been attempting to force synergy into your system. Teamwork is a product that develops from other sources within your team. Conversely, a lack of teamwork is a symptom, it manifests to expose sources of dysfunction within your organization. At its foundation, teamwork is a product of trust.

Trust Springs From The Head Of The Fountain

When trust is built into the structure of a team, teamwork can thrive. Without trust, teamwork will be cyclical at best and will not be able to establish roots within the organization. In the process of building a team, trust has to be a core value from the top down.

A few questions that will help reveal whether there is a foundational trust issue include:

Does leadership trust each other?

Is the leadership team setting an example of trust?

Leaders who believe in the vision, who respect their co-workers and promote the beauty of both will organically transfer a level of trust throughout the organization. Leaders who have not bought into the vision and/or have reservations about the trustworthiness of their coworkers will emit a level of distrust that will hinder the development of unity in the organization.

Trust Starts With Trustworthy People

Does your hiring process seek and add trustworthy people to the organization? Employees are watching the hires that you make. Who and how of a company's hiring process enhances or undermines the culture that your team is trying to build. Is there consistency in how leadership deals with core issues that test the building of trust within the team?

The working measure of trust in the workplace is, "Can I trust you to do what you say?" When a team member commits to performing a task, regardless of how simple or complex, can the other members of the team trust that their teammate will do their best to follow through on their commitments? Stephen Covey puts it well when he says,

> "Contrary to what most people believe, trust is not some soft, illusive quality that you either have or you don't; rather, trust is a pragmatic, tangible, actionable asset that you can create."

Trust Builds Momentum Through Consistency

People that may not have the strongest interpersonal relationships can still work with each other, if they have trust. When there is a disturbance in the force, when leadership is asking why teamwork is scant, the investigation trail should be aimed at sources of trust/mistrust within the organization.

In the sport of rowing, the smallest person on the boat perhaps has one of the most important responsibilities. The prototypical coxswain is 120 pounds and, according to Daniel James Brown's book Boys in the Boat about the University of Washington rowing team that won gold in the 1936 Olympics. He says,

> "From the moment the shell is launched, the coxswain is the captain of the boat. He or she must exert control, both physical and psychological, over everything that goes on in the shell. Good coxes know their oarsmen inside and out —their individual strengths and vulnerabilities—and they know how to get the most out of each man at any given moment. They have the force of character to inspire exhausted rowers to dig deeper and try harder, even when all seems lost."

When your organization is experiencing the effects of low teamwork, the remedy is not to throw more teamwork at the void. Like a good coxswain, you must understand your team so you can address the issues. Stop pretending that the dysfunction doesn't exist or that you know the answers. Start getting to know your team members and sort through the sources that are undermining trust.

Do team members trust each other?

Does management trust employees?

Are we rowing (working) hard but not rowing together?

Trust Flows Or Sputters With Conflict

If teamwork starts with trust, trust survives or dies with truth. Truth fleshes itself in an organization by having a clear vision and bringing people who are invested in seeing that vision through. Truth can be a source of conflict. When conflict is brought about by a tangling among team members over truth, this interaction can be a constructive encounter and must be managed properly to net a positive result.

A commitment to truth, the development of trust, and the momentum of teamwork are all ingredients that must be intentionally maintained over the life of a team. Every organization says that they desire unity. Synergy will only result where teamwork is demonstrated and trust is protected.

Are you an example for your team as to what teamwork looks like?

Do your words and your actions establish the parameters for trust within your organization?

The next time you have concerns or issues with teamwork, take a look at where trust is being built and where it is being undermined in your organization. Build trust by creating clarity around truth in your organization, consistently protecting those values, and developing accountability within the team; from the top down and the bottom up. The first place to look when seeking to build trust, regardless of your position, is to ask whether you are exemplifying or undermining trust in the organization.

"Be true..."

This emphasis on authenticity is important for individuals as well as organizations. Yet, if you are failing or heading towards decline, it takes a strong person to admit they need assistance. In the rapidly evolving market everyone must be acutely aware that what worked last month may not net the same result this month. The need to adapt and adjust to the market is constant. Failure to recognize this reality is a recipe for certain failure.

Our values should be set in stone, insofar as they reflect our ethics and core culture, but our approach to the needs of our clients must be fluid. Lex Sisney shares more on how we remain true to ourselves and yet flexible, "If you want to scale your business successfully — without sacrificing innovation, core values, or execution speed as things get more complex — you'll need to design on principles, not policies."

Good leadership recognizes the survival of the fittest, which isn't so much that the strongest and richest survive but those who are most **adaptable** to their surroundings. Recent history has shown how industry giants have been toppled by rigidity and replaced by entities that were willing to change their approach with the fluctuations of the market.

Clarity comes from truth.

Collaboration comes from a willingness to receive input.

By combining clarity with collaboration, leaders, teams, and organizations will unlock the capacity to compete.

Rigid flexibility

Being yourself and building an authentic company are not unreachable philosophical dreams. A leader who is **listening** will reap the benefits of real time feedback so that their team can adjust course expediently. Jack and Suzy Welch address innovation in this way, "It can and should be a continual, ongoing, normal thing. It can be and should be a mindset that has every employee at every level of the organization thinking as they walk in the door every morning, "I'm going to find a better way to do my job today."

Leaders who understand themselves can create teams and cultures that thrive. Competing in the market requires a strong identity with adaptability. My father in law wisely calls this rigid flexibility. Stay true to your core and nimble enough to adjust to the tides. Have a vision, work tirelessly to execute on your mission but don't get so transfixed that you are unable to adapt.

Six Keys to Positive Organizational Conflict

Whenever you are dealing with people there will always be issues. Even good people have disagreements. The issue with disagreements is not in having them but in how we conduct ourselves. Professionals need to remain professional in how they disagree. Being professional doesn't mean that at times our humanity expresses itself in negative ways (as discussed in the first three chapters), but this should be the exception rather than the norm. Conflict is not the issue.

Proactive conflict resolution

In times of conflict, you will have to decide how directly involved you will need to be in the restoration process. More often than not, it is better for you to acknowledge and address an issue than to ignore it. Our friends from Step Up 2 Success joined us for the The DYOJO Podcast[36] to discuss how developing a better people process leads to better outcomes for all. They specialize in resources for classroom management which have direct application to the workplace. A strong organizational culture will be proactive in preventing negative outbursts. Handling conflict constructively will enhance your efforts to build a positive culture.

Constructive Conflict

Conflict is neutral, it's how you handle it that determines whether it is negative or positive. When team members are able to disagree and work through questions related to vision and value, energy is released that is conducive to progress. In being proactive an organization should establish resources and conditions for how disagreements are addressed so that they can be resolved in a productive manner.

Practical Conflict Boundaries

For example, if two technicians in the field have a disagreement they should understand that it would be improper to carry that confrontation out in front of the customer. A more constructive location for conflict is to go to the truck to work through a disagreement; out of earshot of the client. If the issue is escalating beyond their ability to address it in a constructive manner, then those team members should dismiss themselves from the jobsite to "get lunch" or "pick up materials" so that they can work through their issue.

Management Conflict Engagement

Management should be available to assist as needed when conflict is unresolved between team members. When you hire crew members that embrace and enhance your organizational culture, these types of outbursts should be the exception rather than the norm. Your recruitment and hiring practices should be in line with your organizational values. Misaligned hiring processes undermine your culture.

Organized Conflict

Weekly or monthly team meetings are a great place for team members to work through ideas as a group. If there are issues with performance, productivity, or personalities, these group gatherings can be a proactive method for teaching and training on values as well as conflict resolution. Even when you hire recruits who embrace your culture, you still need to invest in training them and developing your team around those core principles. You should never assume that people will understand or embrace your culture, you need to be clear and consistent in developing it.

The Rules of Conflict

When an employee observes a team member doing something wrong or incorrect, the training and culture should be such that conflict is expected. Employees should be empowered to address each other directly, this is the highest form of sustainable accountability. It will only happen after you have been clear in communicating your values as well as consistent in developing and defending your culture. Depending on the severity of the infraction observed, employees should know when to notify their supervisor. If things escalate or are unresolved then supervisors should be engaged in either re-training or restoring relationships between employees.

There will be conflict.

Will there be solutions?

Your job is to distinguish between constructive and destructive conflict. To be intentional about enhancing rather than undermining the development of your culture. The questions you need to ask as a person in a position of leadership are:

Does the situation of resistance reveal someone who has made a mistake, someone who is processing the changes, or someone who has decided to be an obstacle to progress?

The most effective means of conflict resolution are to prevent conflict. Prevention measures should be built into recruiting, hiring, training, and discipline for the whole organization. The goal is to clarify your vision and values and to build those into everything you do as a team. If you can be clear, you can be consistent and from consistency you can develop accountability.

CHAPTER 16

*The Mindset and Habits of a
Collaborative Culture*

By Jon Isaacson

D oes running your company ever feel like you're playing Jenga? In business you have to make difficult decisions. Whenever the stress and/or consequences of those actions nears a boil and you ask yourself why you keep doing this, you and your management friends remind each other, "That's why they pay us the big bucks."

Note, *big* is italics because it's relative, isn't it?

To win at Jenga, you want to pull pieces from the vertical tower that set your fellow players up for failure. In this game, it is inevitable that the structure will fall. To be triumphant, you want your opponents to be holding the piece that causes everything to finally crumble.

Unfortunately, too many people in a position of leadership treat their own organizations in this same way. Rather than work for the good of all, many are working for their own interests. While self preservation is a trait that runs through all of us, there are those who become blinded by it. You may be tempted to ascribe ill-intent to those who act only in their own self interest but it also can be the result of learning these habits from others and an unwillingness to break the mindset that feeds these negative practices.

I first heard about the parable of *The Two Wolves* at war within each of us from Rachel Stewart's amazing book *Unqualified Success*. It's a story often attributed to the Cherokee or Lenape oral traditions. In short a wise grandfather tells his grandson that inside of him are two wolves that are battling each other. One is darkness and despair, or for our purposes - self preservation; the other is light and hope, or working for the greater good. The grandson asks his grandfather which of the warring wolves inside him will win?

You cannot reach a position of leadership without having had your share of bad managers. Everyone teaches you something, either their negative example reveals what you should not do and what does not work, or their positive example demonstrates how a person in a position of leadership should treat their people as well as lead their teams.

Going back to *The Two Wolves*, which management example will win when you rise to a position of leadership? The wise grandfather answers his grandson's question of who will win with this rousing statement, "The one you feed." Regardless of your managerial *nature* or the organizational environments in which you were *nurtured*, you have to decide which mindset and which habits you will feed.

If you are in business, your organization is like a Jenga tower, so many external forces are continually pulling at the blocks of your company and ready to see it crumble that you do not need to be perpetuating internal strife that adds to those pressures. Most great civilizations have disappeared into history not because they were conquered by their enemies (external) but by being torn apart from within (internally). If you as a person in a position of leadership, do not seek, do not listen, and do not receive input from every level of the organization you will notice that team members become silent.

This silence is a result of your team members coming to the conclusion that either you do not care about making positive changes or that you are not capable of them. Your mindset and habit of self preservation will result in a culture of self preservation. The Jenga tower will fall because everyone is trying to set someone else up to be the one holding the piece that makes the tower (your organization) crumble. You can be upset that your people are acting this way, but because you have been feeding the wrong wolf within yourself, they have learned from your example and now your company is full of the wrong kind of wolves.

The Greater the Challenge the Greater the Need for Collaboration

I was so excited this past year when I was asked by a local organization to give the commencement speech for their statewide conference. As was the case for most of these large in-person gatherings, the event was moved to an online platform. The leadership team for the Washington Association of Maintenance and Operation Administrators (WAMOA) pivoted to make the best of the changing conditions of 2020.

It is quite different preparing for sharing concepts through Zoom as opposed to being in a room where you can feel the pulse. As I structured content that I thought would translate, I thought about what my friend, Idan Shpizear, who is the CEO of one of the fastest scaling property restoration franchises in the United States, shared when he was a guest on The DYOJO Podcast. On episode 34, Idan discussed how he had to learn something important for himself and his growing company,

> *"Often we OVER estimate what we can accomplish in ONE year,*
> *but UNDER estimate what we can achieve in FIVE to TEN years."*

He is not the author of this prescient quote, but he has proven this concept as he has taken his business, 911 Restoration, from lugging around a portable carpet cleaner in an undersized 1978 Volvo with 100,000 miles on it to a company grossing over $50 million in 2015.[37] I am not sure if you can comprehend the difficulty of regularly loading and unloading a commercial carpet cleaning from the backseat or side door of a Volvo, but it definitely would not be ideal. Carpet cleaning itself is labor intensive, having an ill fitted vehicle adds another layer of complexity to the process. Yet, they fed the entrepreneurial wolf that told them that together they could do it.

Have you heard, or used, the statement, "Control what you can control"? When you really take some time to think about it, and in the ups and downs of 2020, time to think has been something everyone had a little TOO MUCH of, you realize there is VERY LITTLE that we can control. The fallout from the COVID-19 pandemic and response has made all of us question the illusion of control even more.

And yet, we are still here.

WAMOA was not able to carry out their plans for a physical event that so many were looking forward to in beautiful downtown Yakima, Washington. But that reality did not stop the resolve of their leadership team. The show must go on, as they say, even if the show is different than it has ever been. The WAMOA wolf may not have howled as proudly as it had in previous years, but they fed the networking wolf that told them they could do it.

Idan and his partner Peleg Lindenberg came to the United States with a dream and $3,000 to their names. $800 of that was spent on the run-down Volvo. They didn't have an elaborate business plan but they knew they needed to get to work. If you are reading this, you are one of the many growth minded professionals who are continuing to make the best of whatever curve balls life has thrown at you.

While we know that we will survive 2020 and beyond, it takes vision and courage to press forward in the face of your obstacles. Every year, every month, and every day brings new challenges. I want to encourage you to remember Idan's words, "Often we overestimate what we can accomplish in one year, but underestimate what we can achieve in five to ten years."

This quote encourages our mindset for how we will cross the "finish" line for 2021 and beyond. You are moving forward and you are going to control what you can control. You are going to feed the wolf of collaboration, but before you can do that effectively, we have to undue many years of the wrong mindset and habits of leadership.

The Habits of Leadership In Uncharted Territory

WAMOA's vision statement is one that resonates with all organizations - *Developing successful facility leaders through professional collaboration.* Whatever the fallout from COVID-19 throws at us, it does not take away our responsibility, our calling, or our ability to, "Develop successful _____ (fill in the blank for you industry) leaders through professional collaboration?"

That organization's 2020 president, Marina Tanay, from Sumner Bonney Lake School District in Washington State, has stated her vision as, "Leading by action and example." She was elected to the role because she is a visionary and she works hard to live out that vision statement. To her it is not aspirational, it is actionable. She shared a quote that drives her mindset and habits from Donald H. McGannon,

"Leadership is not a position or title. It is action and example."

Speaking of what we can accomplish, even in the face of 2020's challenges, we recently experienced this outpouring of support for our First Annual The DYOJO Podcast Socktember Sock-Raising Event to Support Local Charities[38]. Our inaugural event was a great success with the impassioned participation of the following team leaders, sponsors, and their motivated teams:

Lindsey Ward (Contents Specialists of Washington)
Tammy Birklid (Merit Construction)
Jon Isaacson (3 Kings Environmental)
Kelsey Isaacson (Home with Kelsey Isaacson)
Luke Draeger (Aramsco Seattle).

Collectively **we were able to raise over 5,500 new pairs of socks** as Lindsey and her Sisters for Socks teams took the 2020 #socktember trophy with the highest number of socks raised.

I want to challenge you to think about development in terms of *The Ladder Mindset vs. The Mountain Mindset*. Remember, the wolf that you feed inside of you will be the wolf that grows. If you want to enhance collaboration in your organization you need to identify and eliminate those mindset and habits that undermine your efforts to build a strong culture.

The Ladder Mindset:

How many times have you thought about personal or professional development in terms of "climbing the ladder?" Too often we limit our organizational and personal vision by conforming to the mindset and habits of the *leadership ladder*. There is tremendous pressure to follow the status quo, as we think it is safer to do so. But when you take a step back and see how this commonly held mindset leads to consistent dysfunction, such as the self-destructive Jenga habits, you must feed a different wolf if you want a different result.

Think for a moment, what is the view like when everyone is on the same ladder trying to reach "the top"?

The Ladder Mindset:

On a ladder, there is a limited view and therefore limited opportunities.

On a ladder, the perception is that there is always someone above, regardless of how far someone climbs.

On a ladder, team members feel like they are either being stepped on or pulled down.

The Ladder Habits:

On a ladder, there's only one "top spot", so there is little room for collaboration; it all but ensures conflict.

On a ladder, those with unique skills, perspectives, and abilities feel limited by their chances to contribute to the mission.

If you are in a position of leadership and you have the ladder mindset, you will perpetuate:

A limiting view of opportunities and challenges.

A bottleneck of upward mobility and idea flow.

A challenge in getting your team members to collaborate.

The one thing everyone fears when going on a ladder is falling off of said ladder. Jenga is a game where pieces are extracted from the structure until the inevitable happens; the tower falls. In human interactions, we all have a bent towards self preservation. As a person in a position of leadership, if you want to have a shot at altering this downward spiral for your team, you have to develop a new mindset as well as new habits, for yourself and your organization.

The Mountain Mindset:

In the Pacific Northwest we are so blessed to have beautiful views. After over three years of living back in the South Sound, the name locals use to refer to the areas below Seattle, I am still captivated by breathtaking views of Mount Rainier. Wherever you are from, picture a picturesque local climbing trail or nearby mountain, what are the views along the upward trail from those landmarks?

On a mountain, there are no limits to the views (opportunities).

On a mountain, there are many ways to get to "the top".

On a mountain, the more challenging the climb the more we need our team mates to help us overcome and work through obstacles (collaboration).

The Mountain Habits:

On a mountain, the "top spot" is only one of many desirable opportunities.

On a mountain, there are unlimited success trails and collaboration enhances progress for the team.

On a mountain, there is plenty of room for people with unique skills, perspectives, and abilities to contribute to the mission.

If you are in a position of leadership and you have the mountain mindset, you can:

Create an unlimited view of opportunities where team members embrace challenges together.

Help the best ideas flow throughout the organization as your team recognizes that obstacles require everyone to work together to achieve your shared big hairy audacious goals (BHAGs).

Build collaboration and creativity to help the mission move forward.

With this renewed perspective, progress, rather than position, becomes the goal. As we have said many times, the four pillars (the blueprint) of success are people, process, production and progress. If you are committed to advancing professionalism and excellence, that isn't done because of your position, it is accomplished, as Marina shared, "By action and example."

When you are intentional with your mindset and your habits, you shift yourself into a place where you aren't limiting your team and fostering dysfunction. When you lead by example you are enhancing your opportunities to make progress. Developing the right mindset and habits are important because:

Your mindset affects your habits

Your habits affect your production

Your production affects your progress

Your progress affects your mindset

Within the mountain mindset team members are empowered

to find unique roles that unlock their creativity at work. This culture enhances the spirit of working for the good of all rather than being funneled into a system that rewards a limited range of success parameters. Taking even a few small steps in the right direction is worth more than thousands of busy steps in the wrong direction.

Developing a Collaborative Mindset

The authors of this book believe that culture is a competitive advantage. Attracting, hiring, and retaining good talent is a differentiator between companies that build sustained success and those that flounder. In Chapter 3, I noted that my goal was to demonstrate three things with regards to your efforts to develop your culture, that they are:

Worthwhile

Within your realm of control

Less complicated than you think

This is a book by everyday people in positions of leadership, for everyday people in positions of leadership. As awesome as my friends are, this book will not solve all your problems, but hopefully you will understand that first, you are not alone in your quest and second, you have a network of people who are willing to help you achieve your goals.

I hope that we have proven that:

Taking care of your culture is critical to taking care of your people.

Taking care of your people is essential to taking care of your customers.

Taking care of your customers is the foundation of a sustainable business.

Developing, adapting, and caring for your culture is vital to your vitality as an organization. Your **input** of time, effort, and resources towards developing an intentional culture is directly linked to achieving optimal business **outputs**. Another distinguished person in a position of leadership from the property restoration industry, Marion Wade, who is the founder of the now billion dollar company ServiceMaster, said, "Don't expect to build a super company with super people. You must build a great company with ordinary people."

In positions of leadership, we have to constantly ask ourselves if our lack of progress is baked into the processes we are creating or managing. It is difficult to make deep changes when job security is often tied to maintaining a system rather than taking a step back in order to take multiple steps forward.

Success is not easy or guaranteed. But each of us has the ability to chart a path to progress. You may not have the ability to control sweeping changes, but are you making the changes that are within your control? Culture is key to collaboration and your culture is a reflection of your shared mindset and habits. Those in a position of leadership make the most progress when they harness the power of leading by example.

> In your own mindset, are you stuck trying to climb the leadership ladder or are you tackling the mountain?

> Are you cultivating habits for your team that are limiting the flow of ideas and choking collaboration, or are you opening pathways to reduce dysfunction and unlock the creativity of your team members?

Developing Collaborative Habits

What we believe will shape how we act. If you believe that you are powerless, you will be. If you believe that you cannot achieve, you won't. Perhaps you feel like you are stuck in a rut. I believe that Idan's encouragement will empower you to think about things a bit differently and therefore act a bit differently.

As a practical application, maybe we take Idan's words and break that down further, "Often we overestimate what we can accomplish in one year, but underestimate what we can achieve in five to ten years."

What about ONE month vs. FIVE months?

What out ONE week vs. FIVE weeks?

What about ONE day vs. FIVE days?

We are all dealing with a laundry list of challenges, similar to Idan's start up story, which included limited funds, battered resources, and tired bones. In a collaborative environment we are rowing together in the right direction. Often our lack of progress as an organization is not a result of a lack of effort but rather a lack of clarity in our direction and consistency in our ability to work together. If three people in a boat are rowing as hard as they can, the work ethic is there but the vessel is spinning in circles.

By communicating with your team as you develop your culture, you clarify the vision and values that empower you all to work together towards your goals. When you stop feeding the chaos, you can start the process of unleashing collaboration.

What are the First Steps Towards the Mountain Mindset?

Update your INPUTS, get around people who talk about opportunities rather than commiserate about obstacles.

Update your VIEW of your situation. It is much harder to climb a mountain than a ladder, but it is also much more exciting and rewarding.

Update your MINDSET. Revise your one year plan and broaden your five year goals.

Update your HABITS. Get off the ladder and start training, preparing, and gathering a team to tackle the mountain.

CHAPTER 17

Garbage In, Garbage Out (Part 2): The Imperial Order of the Work Order

By Jon Isaacson

Manager 1 complains, "I can't get my workers to stop going to the hardware store multiple times in a day."

"How detailed are your work orders?" Friendly neighborhood restoration coach asks.

Let's discuss how an organization can align their processes with their vision to ensure they are not undermining their goals. We will take a trip down memory lane and construct this chapter in the fashion of the *Choose Your Own Adventure Series* paperbacks that were popular in the 90s.

I believe that I am a bridge millennial. I am technically Gen Y but I believe that my perspectives and experiences are more in line with Gen X. With The DYOJO Podcast, my goal has been to help growth minded professionals to shorten their DANG learning curve, which often requires listening to and learning from those who have *been there, done that* (BTDT) and lived to tell others about it. By utilizing a structure that will bring some nostalgia to 90s kids, let's see if we can unpack some of these common dysfunctions in the skilled trades.

How do you think Manager 1 answers the question we posed

above regarding work orders?

> A. ""What's a work order?" - *advance to paragraph 1*
> B. "They're pretty good. Why are you busting my butt?" - *advance to paragraph 2*
> C. "I'd like to see how Company X does theirs any better. Give me a break." - *advance to paragraph 3*
> D. "Flawless." - *advance to paragraph 4*

Paragraph 1 - Definition of a Work Order

"What's a work order?"

Define a work order: what should be in it and why it is important.

One of my first articles, actually my second one, submitted to Restoration and Remediation Magazine, was a little expose titled *Peeling Back the 5 Layers of Communication in a Restoration Business*[39]. In this chapter we dug into the many layers that contribute to a customer calling your office wondering what the heck is going on with their project. Another common dysfunction in the skilled trades.

I will ask for forgiveness later, but I am going to do something taboo and quote myself,

"In order to fix this, we will need to address the system from top to bottom and will need every layer of our organization to be invested in the restoration of our process. Communication is our organization showing our customers that we value them. Clarity and consistency is our organization showing our employees that we value them."

In order to achieve the ever-coveted, rarely-achieved accountability in your organization, we have to communicate clearly and consistently at every level of your organization. In the 5 Layers we discussed:

Clarity at the point of work intake

Clarity at the point of work initiation

Clarity within the organization

Clarity within your work communication

Younger readers may be surprised that even in 2010, I arrived at one of the largest restoration companies in our industry and they were still using carbon copies for hand written work orders. There is nothing wrong with old tech: use what you have and make it work. But, if your handwriting is illegible (which is the case for most people in the skilled trades), then you're not setting your team up for success if you are creating work orders that no one can read.

We quickly adapted our process to printed work orders which were much easier for everyone to read. As we added team members who were more tech-savvy than me, we further adapted our work orders and scheduling to Google calendar. I can tell you that we tried almost every app and software available at the time and found most of them took more time to manage than the actual work.

The shared calendar allowed us to put job relevant information into the hands of those serving our clients. A good work order does not have to be complex, but it must contain key details such as customer name, contact information, jobsite address, scope of work, and should even include budgeted time so that your team has a target to shoot for.

Now that you know what a work order is, you will want to *advance to paragraph 2* to learn about creating clarity and/or *advance to paragraph 4* to learn about developing consistency in your process.

Paragraph 2 - The Importance of Clarity

"They're pretty good. Why are you busting my chops?"

In order for a work order to be effective, it needs to be clear enough to provide the details necessary for the receiver to be able to work from the orders. When the person assigned to the work reads the document they should be able to comprehend the following:

What am I going to be doing?

Where am I going to be doing this work? This includes the location of the job as well as the areas where work is and isn't to be conducted.

What materials, tools, and/or equipment will I need in order to accomplish the tasks assigned?

Are there any special or specific items that I need to address?

How much time do I have budgeted to complete this work?

It is important for people in a position of leadership to keep in mind that the goal of a work order is to communicate with the person(s) who will be assigned to complete the work assigned. It is not enough to document what the writer thinks is clear; those composing the work orders must work to ensure the information can be understood and executed by those on the receiving end of the transmission.

I heard a great analogy in regard to instructing a child to clean their room.

Parent: "Clean your room."

Child: "Ok."

Fifteen minutes later the parent returns and finds that the child has not cleaned their room to the parent's satisfaction. Who is at fault for this failure? Many managers, and parents, might say,

Parent: "It's common friggin sense, what's wrong with you child?"

If you are in agreement while you read this segment of the article - *advance to paragraph 1.*

If we take it seriously that effective communication requires those in a position of leadership to work at clearly and consistently transferring information, then we can clearly see that the child was not set up for success in the scenario above.

George Bernard Shaw aptly states, "The single biggest problem in communication is the illusion that it has taken place."

So, what should the "clean your room" work order look like in order to enhance the opportunity for a better outcome?

Parent: I want you to clean your room. By this I mean, I want all of your clothes put away or in the dirty clothes hamper, your toys put away in their bins, and your bed made nicely. I will return in fifteen minutes to check on your progress. Do you understand what I have instructed you to do?

If you are ready to work on improving the process, *advance to paragraph 4*.

Paragraph 3 - The Illusion of Competition

"I'd like to see how Company X does theirs any better. Give me a break."

Why would it matter what other companies are doing? If the bar is low among your competitors, making yourself feel good about your own lack of clarity doesn't solve anything to prove that you are on par with the status quo. You are in competition with yourself. Your ability to make progress towards your goals is dependent on your ability to motivate yourself, your management team, and your technicians to raise the bar internally for your organization.

It's time to *return to the start* and select the answer that most closely reflects your thoughts on the matter. For example, if you are deflecting because you don't actually know what a work order is, *advance to paragraph 1*.

Paragraph 4 - Developing the Process

"Flawless."

If this is true, why is it that you are not getting the results that you seek in reducing waste by curbing the unnecessary trips to the hardware store that opened our story? You may believe that your communication is clear, but this dysfunction is revealing that there is still work to be done either in truly creating clarity in your work order (paragraph 2), developing consistency in your process (paragraph 5), or holding people accountable through a plan of improvement (paragraph 6).

I have written at length on the process of developing the right mindset and habits for yourself and your team to succeed with estimating insurance claims in my first book, Be Intentional: Estimating. If you have a desire to dig further into these principles, as well as prepare your team to communicate scope more effectively from the estimating stage onward, you may find this publication to be of value.

To review the scope communication process *advance to paragraph 5*.

If your work order process is clear, as outlined in paragraph 2, and you have developed a consistent process, as outlined in this section, it may be time to move into the discipline phase. If it's time to discipline - *advance to paragraph 6*.

Paragraph 5 - Establishing Accountability

Whenever information has to translate from an estimator, to a project manager (sometimes one in the same), to a site supervisor, or carpenter, your scope communication process must be clear and consistent before employees can be held accountable.

A work order, as defined in paragraph 1, is a transfer of critical information so that all parties are clear on the scope of work. Before you can hold team members accountable for multiple trips to the hardware store, you must confirm whether they have been set up for success at the project start up.

It's one thing when management holds people accountable, it's another thing when team members understand the vision and values and are empowered to hold each other accountable.

The author of *Necessary Endings*, Dr. Henry Cloud, has said,

"If you are building a culture where honest expectations are communicated and peer accountability is the norm, then the group will ad-

dress poor performance and attitudes."

Many years ago, my beautiful wife went to work with my team on several large school projects. We needed people we could trust to do what they were instructed by the team. My wife was more than capable. She worked well with the team and has some fond memories of her time with people who stand out as some of the best that I have worked with over my career. They weren't the smartest or the most talented, in truth, we assembled a rag-tag group of people who fought for each other and worked hard to *do it right.*

One cool story that came out of the experience was my wife seeing more of what went on behind the scenes. She confirmed what I already knew, that our team was committed to doing it right, doing it efficiently, and doing it excellently. Because our process was clear and consistent, the team held each other accountable to the standard that we all believed in. I am reading *The ServiceMaster Story* by Albert M. Erisman, in which he has a great quote from the founder Marion Wade,

"Don't expect to build a super company with super people. You must build a great company with ordinary people."

If you want accountability, focus on clarity (paragraph 2) and then build consistency in your process (paragraph 4). Even if you have an accountable team, there will be times when you have to discipline - *advance to paragraph 6.*

Paragraph 6 - Effective Discipline

This book is my second. It has been a longer process that I anticipated. I am proud of the results of this collaborative effort with several talented authors who have been there, done that (BTDT) and lived to tell about it. Our goal is to share real world experiences with those mindsets and habits that either enhance or undermine your efforts to build on your vision and values. In the opening chapters I discussed how those in a position of leadership need to understand that in many ways people are like banks - you have to make emotional deposits (credits) if you want to effectively make emotional withdrawals (debits).

As a person in a position of leadership, you often have to address issues in your organization (correction). Before you can build or expect accountability in your culture, you must build a foundation of clarity and consistency:

> Be clear and teach your team to *do it right.*

> Build consistency and help your team to *do it efficiently.*

> Develop accountability and show your team how to *do it excellently.*

If we return to our opening scenario, our manager, like many people in a position of leadership, is frustrated by a clear example of waste. When workers make multiple trips in a day to the hardware store, you are losing on so many fronts. You are losing productivity, money, trust, and the list goes on. Lisa Lavender and I recently teamed up to share some thoughts on reducing common areas of scope creep[40] in property restoration.

In our market, a trip to the hardware store consumes at least one hour. If you can reduce one trip to the hardware store, you gain one hour of productivity. Over the course of a week that is five hours of productivity gained. That's almost an entire shift that your worker is either losing or gaining productivity.

Before we can put all of the blame on our worker, people in a position of leadership have to face the music and ask themselves whether they have created a process of communication that is clear, consistent, and thereby facilitates accountability. We are quick to use, "Garbage in, garbage out," as an indictment against our technicians when this responsibility starts with the organization, the management team, and the internal processes of the company before it ever reaches the ground floor.

Remember the following,

> <u>People in a position of leadership are responsible for:</u>
> Clarity
> Consistency
> Accountability

<u>Team members must learn to:</u>
Do It Right
Do It Efficiently
Do It Excellently

CHAPTER 18

Small Things That Enhance Culture

By Jon Isaacson and Multiple Contributors

Several years ago I reached out to multiple people in a position of leadership that I respected for having made significant effort to build a positive culture in their organizations. If you have a similar resolve, you know that the work is never done. I didn't complete the whole series but the first two articles brought out the power of two simple to implement, and highly effective, resources:

The importance of listening to your team and the power of encouragement.

Creating a good working environment is not an easy task but it should be the goal for any company that wants to remain competitive in the current market where finding good people is often more difficult than finding good customers. When we reached out to multiple leaders across various industries, we found one ingredient that is key to developing a team that operates in the positive margins of employee engagement is the simple art of listening.

Use Your Ears to Create Value

Danny Morgan, who is a store manager for a national retailer in Eugene, Oregon, shared, "I can tell you it's not about the money no matter what they say, we all work for the money but it's not about the money – ain't about the fetti." So if it isn't about the money, what can leaders do to ensure they are communicating to their employees that they are invested in them as people? Mr. Morgan told us, "Every moment to listen, every second of praise and every time letting them know that they can come to you with anything knowing that you will provide a positive spin or reaction." Listening to team members shows them that they are worth our time and that we care to hear what they have to say. Employees may not always come to you when it's convenient, but it is important to remember to make time for them as what they share may not seem important but it could be critical to them.

> *There is really no substitute for experience. You must have experience and be open to experience — that helps. That helps a lot. Most importantly, you have to be yourself, be who you are and take time to be open and honest with yourself. That is what it's all about. If you don't know yourself, you'll never have great style. You'll never really live. To me, the worst fashion faux pas is to look in the mirror, and not see yourself. - Iris Apfel*

Randy Carley, Water Damage Restoration Specialist, Washington

You catch a lot more flies with honey, than you do with vinegar. Asking with a "please" and always saying "thank you" goes incredibly far in delegating, especially when you're asking for something no one is volunteering to do.

As for a "negative"

"It's not my job..."

Four words that show someone's true colors. This mentality is alive and well despite companies' efforts towards their culture. Sadly, it's also still being kept alive by managers who may not say it anymore, but show it by demanding or assuming a lot, yet they aren't willing to roll up their sleeves and help.

"Great things are done by a series of small things brought together." - Vincent Van Gogh

Tatsuya "Tats" Nakagawa, Specified Podcast

Culture is a very important part of your organization. As a former do-it-all entrepreneur, it took me a long time to understand this. I went through most of my entrepreneurial career without creating a well-defined mission, vision and core values statement. As a result, there was no clarity within our organization and not surprisingly this resulted in an ineffective corporate culture.

A friend and fellow entrepreneur introduced me to a series of books (*Rocket Fuel, Traction, Get a Grip*) by Gino Wickman that outline an operating system that would help our organization become more organized and would ultimately help us create the right culture of accountability. Many companies like to use fancy words to describe their culture, but without accountability, every organization will eventually fail.

"Compliments are low cost and high yield investments in your most valuable assets." - Jon Isaacson

Teamwork Starts With Listening

Firefighters know a thing or two about building a team. Teamwork is important to all professions, but it is critical when a group must band together to respond to life and death scenarios. Coy Morris, who fights fires with his team near Seattle, Washington, notes that, "Finding the common goal(s) amongst you and your team requires open and safe conversation." Who initiates the process of establishing common goals and building a culture of open communication? For Mr. Morris, "I think the organization sets the mission, the team balances objectives with reality, but I think it starts with management."

Even though fire-fighting is dangerous, this alone is not enough to forge individuals into a strong team as there are plenty of dysfunctional teams that work in high pressure situations. Many of these teams are able to pull it together when necessary but how much more positive would the environment be if they were able to function cohesively? Danny Morgan reminds us that building respect goes both ways, from leaders to and from employees, "One important thing [to remember] is it takes time, one day at a time."

Listening is the Key to Unlocking Employee Engagement

Tom Los who leads a team for a local government entity in Moses Lake, Washington notes that listening can bring engagement as well as new opportunities for the organization, "I listen to my staff and then give them projects and tasks which mixes their job up. They really enjoy it. If someone has an idea, I try to embrace it as much as possible and let them do it." When people in a position of leadership fail to listen they may be holding the team back from sharing ideas that could solve problems or push the organization forward.

Service industries are built upon the strength of their team members to work together to carry the values of the organization through consistently on every project. Denis Beaulieu who operates in project management leading property restoration and abatement teams in Moorpark, California echoes the importance of listening, "Making sure that they are heard when asked. Have their ideas mean something and not just ask for an opinion or suggestion but try them and see if they work. Don't discount anyone's ideas or make yours more important."

Rex Fox, Retired Facilities Management Executive, Oregon

One thing I did that I believe may have been positive for the CU's culture was to try to get to know everyone who worked at the CU and then when I saw them in the halls or in their branches, I would say hi and try to use his/her name. It's easy to look down, act busy or whatever when you approach others, but a smile and a hello (good morning, how's it going, etc.) along with using the person's name often brightens that person's day just enough to make a difference. It makes work more fun too.

One small thing that helped reduce friction was to not ask or receive reasons for time off. Managers should only be deciding whether they can accommodate a request for time off, not the merit of the reason for the request.

"Help others achieve their dreams and you will achieve yours." - Les Brown

Idan Shpizear, CEO and Author, California

Something that worked very well:

We created a system that gives everyone in the company visibility to what everyone in the company is working on and how they are making progress (including me as the CEO). That empowerment fuels the reality that everyone in the company is important. It empowers people and encourages people to help each other in achieving their goals.

Something that didn't work well:

When we started with the fresh start attitude we wrote everything out and put it on our walls and we thought that this would be enough but just saying it didn't take us anywhere.

"A good working environment will culminate in a culture where everyone is clearly rowing in the same direction." - Josh Gourley

Acting Upon What Your Hear

As noted by many that we interviewed, the catchwords and principles we hear from business leadership books go only as far as we are willing to apply them in our teams. What we want to know from real people who are practicing teamwork, leadership and developing organizations that operate on their values, is how they flesh out these principles in their day to day lives. Denis builds upon his comments from before regarding listening, "Empower people. They feel more a part of the organization when they feel they are part of it and not just working for it. Most important people want to feel they belong."

To be successful in a position of leadership, individuals must remember where they came from, what they desired while they were in the trenches and serve as an intermediary between the makers of decisions (the suits) and the daily decision makers (those in the field). Rex Fox who serves in the leadership team for a credit union based out of Eugene, Oregon, outlines a few key touch points relevant to listening, "Be approachable. Learn about the staff and what is important to them. Be trustworthy and trust your staff (but inspect). Roll up your sleeves and help when needed, but don't do their jobs for them." Rex brings up a great point that when we roll up our sleeves and get our hands dirty being shoulder to shoulder with our team members there is an organic exchange between individuals that cannot be built any other way.

Bring Your Team Together With Your Ears

Listening provides a means to blur the lines between management and employees that often holds a company back from reaching its potential. When a person in a position of leadership takes the time to listen, they remind themselves and the whole team that we are all in this together. Much can be learned about individuals, teams, issues and opportunities by simply taking a moment to hear and receive input from those who are investing in the team, the customers and the culture.

"We never tell anyone no. We tell them this is what we can do." - Kelly Burns

Alex Watts, Senior Area Maintenance Manager, Washington

Years ago, while working as a maintenance supervisor for an apartment community, I identified a corporate legal-liability, with potential for catastrophic fines and penalties. I knew that on a specific date, the companies contractor license was set to expire, due to a job-change by the companies previously assigned administrator. Without a replacement administrator, the contractor license would become null and void. I notified several levels of corporate associates, including my Regional Manager, Regional Maintenance Manager, Director of Maintenance, and additional parties beyond that as well, and I didn't receive a response.

Meanwhile, I took it upon myself to research what was needed to fulfil the vacant position. I registered to test for the required license, passed the test and became the only individual employed in the company who could legally fulfill the administrator position. I notified the same group of leaders of my new status and volunteered to fulfill the administrator-requirement to keep our account active. I reminded everyone that the deadline was fast approaching.

I was not placed into the position. The response I received was not congratulatory or grateful, it was curious; "How did you get the license?"

The contractor license expired... I emailed all parties again, notifying them that a corporate email should be sent, informing everyone that it is now illegal and punishable by fines to perform select job-duties, previously covered by the contractor license. I didn't get a response. No company notification was sent.

The contractor license had been expired for several months, while illegal work was being performed. A corporate email finally came out announcing the new administrator has passed their test and will be taking over the account. It was the same person who asked how I acquired my license all those months ago.

After that, I knew my value in the organization was exclusively to boost those above me. I was not intended to join their ranks. I left and found an organization whose culture was receptive and appreciative of my feedback and initiative.

Now that I am in a national leadership position and have associates from all levels of the organization reaching out to me, I frequently use this experience as a guide. I draw upon the experience to motivate me, to be better, to be a leader, and be a resource for my team.

Simply being present and available can make all the difference in the world. If your leaders are not available to your associates, your company culture is crumbling.

The best advice I can give is this:
If an associate reaches out with a question/concern/recommendation/advice or whatever it may be, respond to their input. While it may not be practical to enact their suggestion, or possible to alleviate the cause of their concern, it is easy to respond and explain the "why" behind the final decision. If you ignore associate inputs, it will be the last you hear from that associate. When associates have no voice, the company has no culture.

"Honest disagreement is often a good sign of progress." Mahatma Ghandi

David Smith, Sales, Oregon

The little things play a huge role in life, personal and professional. Simply being transparent with your team can go a long way toward impacting your culture.

I have experienced working for organizations that approached transparency differently during economic difficulties. A negative experience was during the great recession. The organizations I worked came across as secretive. They told a number of employees raises were coming but as the economy took a turn for the worst, they stopped communicating. The organizations laid people off and those who remained never got a raise. This created panic and uncertainty. It was a few months later that employees found out the organization was on a hire and raise freeze. This negatively affected the culture by creating uncertainty and a sense of togetherness.

Fast forward to the COVID pandemic working for another organization who took a different approach. Instead of being secretive, this organization laid it all out on the table. A company simulcast was called, they were very transparent. They informed us people would be furloughed and those that remained would take a temporary pay cut because of the uncertainty during the pandemic. The organization moved from monthly meetings to weekly ones, discussing how to navigate the pandemic and even shared our financials with all of its employees.

This organization's mission statement focuses on being the one place for all your estimating and bidding needs. This applies to the culture; we are one and that is always a part of our weekly meetings. Everyone in the organization pulled together to exceed expectations during the pandemic. Furloughed employees came back, wages were restored, and salary lossed during the pay reduction was even paid back.

Transparency goes a long way toward impacting your culture. It can bring a team together or tear them apart. As Jim Carrey once said, "The truth shall set you free."

A Good Working Environment in Enhanced by Encouragement

The dynamics of the modern workplace are challenging owners and managers alike. When contemplating the nature of a good working environment, another way of thinking about the nature of the topic is to correlate it with a sustainable working environment. If leaders want to create an organization that will stand the test of time, or even the challenge of tomorrow, they must apply their effort to building a good culture.

While many people in a position of leadership feel lost when navigating the modern workplace environments, citing difficulties connecting with millennial employees, many of the most effective methodologies are also rather simple. We previously discussed the power of listening on creating a good working environment. Now we will discuss the importance of encouragement when building a thriving team.

Encouragement is defined as the action of giving someone support, confidence, or hope. People in a position of leadership (PIAPOL) have to embody and exemplify these values if they want to see them practiced throughout the organization. Too often we are people of extremes, we often engage in some aspect of leadership to the exclusion of others. When addressing topics related to culture, environment and emotional intelligence the instruction provided often gloss over the realities of management. There is a balance between encouragement and expectations so that the team vision, values and purpose are carried through in the real world.

"Vision without execution is hallucination." - Thomas Edison

Brian Wilcut, General Manager, Washington

One of our four Core Values here is "Teamwork". Being a member of a successful team can be very rewarding and pay great dividends both in your personal life as well as during your journey along your chosen career path. As a general manager for our regional facility here in the Pacific Northwest, I strive to embrace my current role as a mentor, an advisor, a coach, and a discrete and confidential consultant. Listening to your team's concerns provides insight into their thoughts on the company culture, operations, and procedures.

Being available to lend an ear and engaging them when providing input, empowers them and makes me a better-informed manager. This goes for clients and vendors as well. Take the time to listen and show that you really care about the successes people have and understand the challenges they are enduring. Most importantly, be genuine to all and true to yourself.

"Optimism is the faith that leads to achievement. Nothing can be done without hope and confidence." Helen Keller

Woody Frame, Service Manager, Washington

One time some time ago we had a "senior tech" that we allowed to pick his calls he wanted to go out to. He was the only one that was allowed to do this in the company. The other technicians noticed this and questioned this practice. It caused the others to be resentful to him and distrust the company and question whether the company was treating everyone fairly. Some left and others stayed but lost the will to better their numbers.

This policy was changed and no one got to see the schedule and stack the cards in their favor. This brought more balance and an equal playing field and brought trust back to the office. In the long run everyone learned how to close more calls and the whole company was not now dependent on one technician. Better in house training and communications also resulted in the outcome.

"You do not need to know precisely what is happening, or exactly where it is all going. What you need is to recognize the possibilities and challenges offered by the present moment, and to embrace them with courage, faith and hope." - Thomas Merton

To Create an Environment of Encouragement, Provide Support.

Management is not about finding a place of luxury within an organization, the role of leadership is to ensure those in their supervision have the clarity, resources and support to achieve success in their roles. Long time insurance agent and business owner Josh Gourley states that success for a team starts with everyone knowing their jobs and corresponding job expectations. The reason Josh believes investing in clarity is that, "A good working environment will culminate in a culture where everyone is clearly rowing in the same direction."

Josh recognizes that in order to lead he must set an example, "What's in my power is leading by example and regular meetings that reinforce the activities and values that make success possible. Managers should be excellent at identifying and acknowledging those activities that move the team in the right direction." When we support those around us we contribute to their success, our collective success and our own, it's a win-win-win.

To Create an Environment of Encouragement, Boost Confidence.

Tom Los who works in city management in the public sector views listening as key to providing opportunities for building confidence with employees. "I listen to my staff and then give them projects and tasks which mix their job up. They really enjoy it. If someone has an idea, I try to embrace it as much as possible and let them do it." Creating a good working environment does not mean that leaders cater to their team without accountability.

Boosting confidence can be accomplished even when a manager has to say no to an idea without de-motivating team members from contributing creative solutions. Tom sees disagreement as an opportunity to provide support, "If I don't see the value in the direction that one of them is proposing, I explain that to them. Sometimes by explaining how much more work it would take and who exactly would be available to manage the change they can see the need to move in a different direction."

Isaac Hodukavich, General Manager, Washington

In 2018, O Bee Credit Union experimented with a new branch design called pub-style banking. The lobby of their new Point Ruston branch was outfitted with brick, brass, and taps from local breweries, just like you might find at your favorite dive bar. Pub-style banking brought O Bee's history as the official credit union of the Olympia Brewery front-and-center in a visceral way. The physical space served to remind members and employees of O Bee's culture.

Marketing programs and slogans do not create culture. I worked for a large financial institution whose mission statement was seriously misaligned with its incentive structure. Its marketing portrayed partnership with its customers. But the employee incentive program demanded sales from each customer. Management pushed employees to sell products and services that the customer did not need or want. The pressure led to bad sales practices that management overlooked. No employees were surprised when the public discovered what was happening and the lawsuits started rolling in.

"Watch your thoughts, they become your words; watch your words, they become your actions; watch your actions; they become your habits; watch your habits, they become your character; watch your character, it becomes your destiny." - unknown

To Create an Environment of Encouragement, Build Hope.

Creating hope encompasses communicating clearly on the vision, being consistent with values and developing a culture where accountability is equired from everyone on the team. Long time pastor Aaron Day notes, "Early on (hiring) let them know what you expect and let them know you will model this (fulfilling the expectations) for them. Acknowledge them when they do and correct them when they don't. If they continue to do well reward (raises, praise, popsicles) if they do poorly, correct, train, discipline, fire."

Even in a faith based or non-profit environment, there is still a purpose and the mission must be carried out for the team to be successful. Clarity, consistency and accountability are as essential for a good working environment for volunteers as well as paid staff. Aaron recommends a book that he says is both good and corny called *Lead For God's Sake* by Todd G. Gongwer. Hope is not something magical, it comes from having a vision and a good environment with encouragement motivates everyone to remain on purpose.

"Optimism is the faith that leads to achievement. Nothing can be done without hope and confidence." Helen Keller

Creating a Good Working Environment Requires Encouragement.

The core principles that lead to a good working environment are simple. That doesn't mean that they are easy, but they cost very little to implement. The difference between being successful in building a good and sustainable working environment is often a few small changes in perspective, effort and follow through. Investing in encouragement, support, confidence and hope is a good place to start.

Author Daniel Goleman analyzed the brain and behavior in relationship to encouragement. In his book *Social Intelligence: The New Science of Human Relationships*, he shares his research results. Belle Beth Cooper recaps such findings in her article published with Fast Company Magazine, "In one experiment, the emotional tone of a leader delivering news to an employee made more impact than the news itself. When negative feedback was delivered with a warm tone, the employees usually rated the interaction positively. On the other hand, good news, such as achieving a goal, delivered with a negative tone would leave employees feeling bad."

"When associates have no voice, the company has no culture." - Alex Watts

Robert More, Environmental Manager, Maryland

One small thing that was a negative for my department's culture was having me as the leader/manager wearing too many hats. It was a disservice to the technicians under me, because I couldn't train them properly or help to pass along the knowledge of performing our work the right way.

I feel that when I was coming up in the industry, as a helper, this was an unhealthy but accepted norm. Unfortunately, it often still is the norm where a new, "green horn", is put in a position to try to handle a loss by themselves. They are thrown into the situation and expected to figure things out on their own with minimal training or direction. We have worked hard to end this vicious cycle, but I recognized that in my overloaded capacity, areas such as training and mentorship fell by the wayside.

It is important for owners to trust their managers and allow them to show you they deserve ownership for their roles and responsibilities. When everything has to be "run up the flagpole" it creates unnecessary bottlenecks which hold up progress.

Owners and managers must be decisive. Indecisiveness becomes a cancer amongst subordinates. We work in high stress environments and a lack of decision making efficiency negatively impacts the stress levels of the team.

A positive area that we have been making progress is, what

Jon Isaacson would call "being more intentional". Napoleon Hill would call "Definiteness of Purpose". We have a morning huddle every morning to go over the schedule and what needs to be done and what we need to get done and how. The owner of our franchise has also become more intentional by setting our company's mission and vision and having our weekly level 10 meeting and Individual Goal Setting and Reviews for us to be more focused and streamlined in our departments and our personal goals.

"It is not a daily increase, but a daily decrease. Hack away at the inessentials." - Bruce Lee

Michael D. Stein, Consultant, Washington

I have two items that may be of interest, if you haven't previously addressed them. While these items are written from the perspective of work, they are applicable (at least for me) in all facets of my life.

Communication.

It has been stated that all of the world's problems can be distilled into two categories: mathematical errors or language errors. I consider math to be a language (a universal one at that!), so I believe the root cause of all issues is simply communications. People frequently use language that is imprecise, and that leads to unintended interpretations; if neither party recognizes that there is an issue, they will continue about their business until it becomes obvious that an issue exists. Imagine two people building a bridge across a river intending to meet in the middle, only to discover that their sections don't line up!

One way to avoid most communications-based errors is to request feedback from the receiving party. That will help ensure everyone understands the situation equally. Additionally, using precise language, while not interesting and thus not appropriate for all venues and/or forms of communication, helps alleviate confusion and ambiguity.

Support.

My passion is helping people develop - to discover and pursue their own goals and passions. I love being involved in developing their careers, strengths, skills, knowledge and understanding, etc. When I work with a person, I am constantly assessing their strengths, weaknesses, likes, dislikes, hopes, dreams, and goals. As I get to learn about each employee, I am constantly trying to provide opportunities to learn new skills, or develop skills they are interested in, and I avoid (whenever possible) exploiting their weaknesses.

Overwhelmingly, I receive very positive feedback from current and previous employees who (for some strange reason) really enjoyed working with me. Perhaps one component, which is critical to the success of my technique, is that I genuinely respect each person working with me, and I take the time to get to know them. That sort of relationship is satisfying for employees, and more productive for the employer.

"Managers tend to blame their turnover problems on everything under the sun, while ignoring the crux of the matter: people don't leave jobs; they leave managers." - Travis Bradbury, co-author of Emotional Intelligence 2.0

Greg Smith, District Manager, Oregon

"Listen to your people."

I have learned this from many years and many personalities. Of course, some are better than others in swaying the leader. The challenge of a leader, in my opinion, is realizing that those that don't speak out, tend to be the ones you need to hear the most. I believe that those that tend to prop themselves up as the spokesman for all, tend to say what they need to say to advance their careers.

There are always more qualified candidates that just don't like the attention and prefer to demonstrate effectiveness vs. talking the talk. It takes a good leader to be patient enough to wait for those results. Especially, with the pressure to show results. Very tempting to take Mr. Good Speaker to an event because it makes you look good vs. getting real data and coaching the right person to step up and take the praise. Even if they are terrified of it.

"Nobody starts out extraordinary. No one begins fully qualified and ready. The minute we understand this principle and it really sinks in, our whole work opens up." - Rachel Stewart, author of Unqualified Success

Robert Rowe, Property Restoration Estimator, Georgia

Below is a sample text, that is easily edited to be saved as email signatures. This allows our team members to produce an easy consistent format for greater communication, transparency, documentation of all work produced. It populates immediately for editing every time you create an email. Obviously you can use this same format for any/all needed trades/roles and levels of responsibility.

Estimator Letter; Introduction:

Hello {Name},

First of all on behalf of {your company name}, let me thank you for the opportunity to help you with your property at {address}. We believe we are the Best in the {City name} Area to handle property cleanup, restoration and related industries and are thrilled you asked us to evaluate your unique situation. Please find attached estimate for {proposed work}.

We have prepared an estimate for the {proposed work}. We have based this estimate upon observations and the report by {person who performed inspection}. Please keep in mind this is an estimate, based upon the best information we have at the present time, and that not everything can be anticipated once work begins and reveals the necessity of perhaps more work or less work than described in the estimate.

We are very confident in our ability to perform all the work. We do feel it encompasses all work presently known to be needed to render a proper {repairs needed}. We do not feel that we can do less than has been estimated with a satisfactory result, and could not incur such a liability, nor would we wish to do less work for you, or only do a portion of the job in order to lessen costs.

If you have any additional questions please feel free to reach out to {Project Manager} for your property or myself.

Again, thank you for the opportunity to help, and please let us know how you wish to proceed.

Sincerely,

{your name}

"Just as you wouldn't put all of your financial eggs in one basket, you also need to diversify your professional relationships."
- Amy C. Waninger, author of Networking Beyond Bias

Gabriel Jones, Restaurant Manager, California

In regards to a minor thing that had a great impact , I learned something from my dad. His style of teaching was that you started with an A, and it was up to you to maintain it. I've adopted his approach to grading with how I view and treat others. Everyone that I come into contact with, I give an A; it is up to them to maintain it. This mentality has given me friendships that by society's standards would deem as odd.

The other side to this is that I've been taken advantage of and experienced brief moments of jadedness; I file these under lessons of discernment. Sometimes someone's second chance is a first impression.

"Be approachable. Learn about the staff and what is important to them. Be trustworthy and trust your staff (but inspect). Roll up your sleeves and help when needed, but don't do their jobs for them." - Rex Fox

Jason Sturgeon, Construction Expert and Instructor, Co-Host of The Critical Path Podcast, Washington

Here is some great advice I received from Jason W. Jones on matters of race and diversity. When approaching something contentious or something you don't understand that you believe will include conflict, start with this phrase: "I'm coming from a place of ignorance."

Beginning tough or complex conversations by sharing that you DON"T know everything, you're probably going to get something wrong, and you need their help to get it right sets the tone for an AWESOME and safe culture.

"Face trouble with courage, disappointment with cheerfulness, and triumph with humility." - Thomas S. Monson

Ken Brown, Community Relations, Oregon

For the last two years the owners have pulled all the employees together. We rented Camp Harlow (Eugene, Oregon) and served breakfast to everyone and then shared with them the expectations we had for every single employee and why.

Last year the theme was being a company of Integrity. We wanted to communicate to our team that in every action, everything you do while wearing a Rexius shirt or driving a Rexius vehicle, do them with honesty and integrity.

This year we spoke of excellence. Asking every employee, no matter what their position was, to do what they do a level higher than ever before. Drive, load, dig, plant, administrate, answer the phone - whatever you do, do it with the highest of excellence.

"Being a great place to work is the difference between being a good company and a great company." – Brian Kristofek

Without oversimplifying the qualities of being a person in a position of leadership, if you are charting a course and moving towards your goals and others are following you, then you are a leader. You won't always be right, but you must be willing to recognize a vision and make a decision (or two). You will be wrong more than once in your lifetime if you dare to lead. When you are intentional, you can adjust your course and adapt as you acquire new information or resources.

If you are reading this, then you have a desire to make progress towards your personal and professional development. You will have enjoyed hearing about an unsung hero who resurrected an icon by following a few simple principles, which we discussed in the chapter on Ted McCarty. We go into greater detail with a few of these leadership concepts in Episode 12 of The DYOJO Podcast, with Mike Kinney and David Smith who are two everyday people in a position of leadership trying to do the right thing, just like you.

Please reach out to myself and/or our talented co-authors and let them know your thoughts on being a person in a position of leadership who is trying to build and enhance your culture. I enjoy hearing and sharing stories from everyday people, like yourself, who are in the trenches making things happen.

AFTERWORD

"Be Excellent to Each Other."

"And party on dudes." These quotes are from "The Two Great Ones", William "Bill" S. Preston Esq. and Ted "Theodore" Logan. You will remember them from their inaugural film, "Bill and Ted's Excellent Adventure" (1989) where two friends travel through history to complete a report, the success of which has implications for the duration of mankind. In this movie, Ted opens a history book and quotes Socrates, "The only true wisdom consists in knowing that you know nothing."

In this book we have worked to share from our experiences what has and has not worked as these people in positions of leadership have labored to build strong cultures in their various organizations. What they know and share comes from trial and error. There is a great quote that I believe is attributed to Debasish Mridha,

> "Experience comes from failure
> and success comes from experience."

If you have found any of the mindsets and habits from our talented authors, it is important to remember that it is not because they are smarter or more talented than you, they likely have more experience than you. If you can learn from their experiences, which many of which have come through surviving and learning from failure, then you can shorten your DANG learning curve. As you pursue building a strong culture, don't make it any more difficult than it has to be. As Bill and Ted put it, "Be excellent to each other." If you are excellent to your people, your people will be excellent to your clients, word will spread and you should have a great shot at remaining competitive as you work with your team to adapt to ongoing challenges and evolutions in the market.

I hope that this book has been structured to be a cohesive read through as well as something that will be a reference when you need some inspiration as you build your team and culture. In the author bio section we have included contact information and relevant websites for our group so that you can follow them and reach out if needed. I have known many of the authors through social media and industry involvement, and have been happy to get to know many of them more deeply as we worked through this process. You will note that many of the co-authors have been guests on my podcast as I have learned a lot from each of them and want the world to hear their great insights on mindset and habits leading to enhancing strong cultures.

If a picture is worth a thousand words, in closing I would like present you with a picture and a few concluding thoughts.

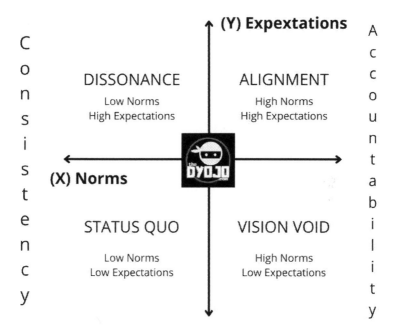

Culture could be described as the culmination of your organizational norms (x - axis) and expectations (y - axis).

Norms are what you do. If you stand back and observe yourself and your team, what do you see? Are your actions in alignment with your stated vision, values, and objectives (or whatever words you use)? As has been stated several times in this book, the question is not whether you have a culture, the question is whether you have been intentional in developing it. Do you communicate your expectations and do the norms you practice and/or allow follow those principles?

Are you, as a person in a position of leadership practicing:

(A) Dissonance
(B) Status Quo
(C) Vision Void
(D) Alignment
(E) Other

Expectations are both those that you declare as well as those that are understood. There often is dissonance between what is done and what is said. Expectations can also be revealed in how you hire, train, discipline, reward, promote, and fire. Similar to parenting, if you say one thing but do another or don't follow through, your team (like children) will continue to test at just how far your boundaries can be pushed.

Does your hiring process include measures to determine if a candidate is a good cultural fit?

How consistently do you train your team on hard and soft skills relevant to your work?

When someone acts out of character for the organization, how are they dealt with?

Consistency is critical to developing norms of behavior that embrace and enhance your culture. How often do we set out to make a change but fail to stick with it long enough to determine whether it is a success or failure and why. I would suggest that you don't make any changes that you are unwilling to commit at least 90 days to the testing of the item's merits. Like a scientist, you should have a thought out hypothesis of what you plan to do, why you think it will work, and how you believe it will affect the team. Most changes have an arc of high investment, low initial productivity, until you get over the "hump" and can see whether the item is going to be effective.

Accountability, from top-to-bottom as well as bottom-to-top, is critical to sustaining and further developing your culture. Expectation means that you are both intentional in your development as well as your communication with your team. Communication in this instance would include training. I recently shared a working definition of accountability that I think is helpful. "Accountability is having a healthy fear that you may be the weakest link on your team and working diligently to ensure that it isn't so." This should not be confused with having a low self-worth or value. What I am attempting to convey is that you want to be on a team of people where you feel a strong desire to ensure you are carrying your weight and others are doing the same. Focus on your roles and responsibilities and work to be the best you can at those. A team helps fill in the gaps only after every individual is 100% committed to mastering their area of contribution.

Status Quo

Low Expectations + Low Norms

You may have a poster on the wall that communicates your "expectations" but in practice there is little communication, training, development, or discipline that reflects, enhances, or defends those stated values. Your norms exist but they are not intentional. Jocko Willink has a great quote, "When setting expectations, no matter what has been said or written, if substandard performance is accepted and no one is held accountable—if there are no consequences—that poor performance becomes the new standard." Too often people in a position of leadership know what needs to be done but don't have the resolve to see things through internal opposition and/or resistance to change. If you aren't disciplined in your own personal and professional development, you are not going to be authentic in your efforts to improve your team. Start by leading yourself so that you can lead by example.

Dissonance

High Expectations + Low Norms

You have the poster on the wall and you have a lot of meetings, but in practice these activities are not intentional or effective at impacting the norms of your organization. I quoted George Bernard Shaw earlier, "The single biggest problem in communication is the illusion that it has taken place." I have been in many organizations where regular "training" occurs but it is rarely designed to address real world scenarios faced by the team members and the standards don't apply to the "money makers" who get a pass on bad behavior. You have to dismount your high horse if you are going to impact change where it matters, at the ground level of your organization. Roll your sleeves up and get some dirt under your fingernails as you work with your team to make positive changes.

Vision Void

Low Expectations + High Norms

Those people in a position of leadership who do very little to develop their cultures and yet somehow have periods of high performing teams, enigmas. The biggest threat in this scenario is for the manager to take too much of the credit for their team's success and not understand who the real drivers of that success have been. Often this type of leader rewards those who they like rather than those who actually contribute and it won't be long before those people get tired of being overlooked. As we have discussed, perhaps *ad nauseum*, in this book - don't make culture more difficult than it is. The beauty of this type of organization is that all that is needed is a bit of investment, of allowing those who shine to formalize the effort, and the people in a position of leadership to defend the culture. When you begin the process of raising the expectations, across the board, to meet the norms, many who have been hiding in the shadows, benefiting from those at the front of the lines, will be revealed and will loudly resist. They may say, "Why mess up a good thing with all these expectations and accountability?" Be brave. Identify and give credit where it is due. This doesn't make you weak as a manager, it will ensure the sustainability of your current high.

Alignment

High Expectations + High Norms

Where your norms meet your expectations, you have alignment of values. There is consistency in your actions and accountability among all of your team members. This doesn't mean that you can let your foot off the gas and coast to victory; far from it. The culture sets the tone and pace, it rallies your team to be disciplined even in periods where motivation may be lacking. All of the items from phases prior apply. You must continue to hire, train, develop, discipline, and fire based upon these expectations and norms (your culture). As you grow and the market changes, you have to adapt. We discussed navigating that curve of growing without losing your values with author Lex Sisney on The DYOJO Podcast Episode 22.

Keep doing good things.

Be intentional.

AUTHOR BIOS

Thank You to These Talented Contributors

In alphabetical order

Acuff, Tiffany

Co-Editor

Technician, Property Restoration

Technician with experience in water mitigation, fire mitigation, mold remediation, contents packing and cleaning, and tarps. Can take a customer from initial loss and lead them throughout the process to the end. I also have experience with back-end tasks, such as getting the proper paperwork and communicating in office with estimators and project managers.

LinkedIn - www.linkedin.com/in/tiffany-acuff-21a525157

Blevins, Michelle

Introduction

Editor in Chief, Restoration and Remediation Magazine

Award-winning journalist and communications specialist dedicated to top-notch, innovative writing to promote my company's brand while fostering strong B2B relationships and spreading knowledge among readers.

Manage all editorial content for Restoration & Remediation magazine.

Creating valuable, quality working relationships with industry professionals.

Write thought-provoking, informative, and educational content for R&R.

Effectively grow the R&R name through brand management via social media, website and other resources.

Manage all social media pages related to R&R including Facebook, Twitter, Google+, & LinkedIn.

Produce weekly eNewsletter containing fresh, relevant content and the latest industry news.

Update and maintain the R&R website including, but not limited to, stories from the latest issue, web-exclusive features, and breaking industry news.

Create relevant video content – including launching two new video segments in the summer of 2015.

R&R is the leading publication for professionals in the restoration and remediation industry. As the thought leader in the restoration world, R&R provides expert information on a variety of topics including forensic restoration, drying, software, thermal imaging, moisture meters, media blasting, and much more.

"Be yourself; everyone else is already taken." - Oscar Wilde

LinkedIn - www.linkedin.com/in/michelle-blevins-821bab22

Author page at R&R - www.randrmagonline.com/authors/2080-michelle-blevins

Michelle Blevins was a guest on The DYOJO Podcast Episode 25

Draeger, Luke

Outside Sales, Aramsco

Outside sales representative for the largest supplier to the abatement and mitigation industries. Specifically, I have extensive knowledge of equipment and supplies pertaining to the disaster restoration field, ensuring I bring a high level of service to Aramsco's valued customers.

A·nom·a·ly: "Something that deviates from what is standard, normal, or expected."

I think this word - "anomaly" - describes me well. An English major with a heart for higher education, I found myself through a series of coincidences in the field of disaster recovery.

For eight years, I supervised and performed mitigation services in homes and businesses, encountering losses large and small. After nearly a decade of 2am phone calls, dealing with insurance claims, consoling homeowners, and swimming in lots and lots of raw sewage, I found I was ready for another challenge.

Through yet another coincidence, I found myself interviewing for the manager job at Interlink Supply of Seattle. The position proved to be one of the most challenging and rewarding of my professional life.

Following the acquisition of Bridgewater (Interink's parent co.) by Aramsco, I am taking on a new challenge as restoration sales manager for the Seattle region.

My approach to sales is unique. We hear all the time that sales is all about relationships, which is certainly true, and I greatly enjoy the relationships I'm able to cultivate each day, but I also think sales is about caring. I think sales is a lot about listening and responding with the heart of a teacher.

My truest passion is for writing. I maintain a blog at legion-writer.com, where I attempt to publish musings at least a few times a month. I also enjoy teaching others to write. I volunteer as a tutor through the King County Libraries.

Some day, that novel I've been pecking away at for six years will see the light. Some day.

LinkedIn - www.linkedin.com/in/luke-draeger-892b4022

Website - www.legionwriter.com

Isaacson, Jon

Host, The DYOJO Podcast

Author, *Be Intentional: Estimating*

For nearly 20 years Jon Isaaacson, The Intentional Restorer, has exemplified consistent achievement in leadership roles within the skilled trades including property restoration, construction, and abatement.

As a business coach, Jon is able to assess issues, identify creative solutions, and implement processes that drive long term success in an organization. You can read his monthly column, *The Intentional Restorer*, in Restoration and Remediation Magazine (R&R).

Jon regularly speaks, writes, and consults through his organization The DYOJO. He is the host of The DYOJO Podcast and recently published his first book *Be Intentional: Estimating*.

LinkedIn - www.linkedin.com/in/jon-isaacson-izvents

Website - www.thedyojo.com

The Intentional Restorer monthly column - www.randrmagonline.com/topics/4576-the-intentional-restorer

The DYOJO Podcast - www.thedyojo.com/listen

Lavender, Lisa

Chief Operating Officer (COO), Restoration Technical Institute (RTI) and Berks Fire Water Restorations, Inc.

Restoration Professional that is passionate about serving others. As Chief Operating Officer of a full service restoration company and training center, manages daily operations so as to deliver services that have a positive meaningful impact on the lives of others.

RTI

Oversees operations of Technical Training center serving restoration, insurance, construction, cleaning and related technical industries. We BELIEVE in inspiring happiness, pride, and innovation in others.

Berks

Oversees the day to day operations of Berks Fire Water Restorations, Inc.ᔆᴹ, a local provider that specializes in the restoration and reconstruction of residential and commercial properties damaged by fire, mold, sewage, smoke, storm, water, wind, or any other damage. Our complete restoration approach involves the coordination and supervision of every facet of the project, ensuring the best possible service. We deal directly with the insurance provider, helping to satisfy the needs of the property owner.

We are fully staffed with a team of restoration technicians, carpenters and tradesmen, providing 24 hour/7 day emergency service with a one hour response time.

LinkedIn - www.linkedin.com/in/llavender

Restoring Success monthly column -
www.randrmagonline.com/topics/4578-restoring-success

Lisa Lavender was a guest on The DYOJO Podcast Episode 36; you can read her monthly column Restoring Success in Restoration and Remediation Magazine (R&R)

McCabe, Andrew

Large Loss Claims Consultant & Xactimate Estimator, Claims Delegates

Author, *The 24 HR Tech*

Andy has spent 20 years in the property damage restoration industry. He is an experienced water damage expert and licensed claims adjuster. He specializes in property damage insurance claims resolution and complex building envelope issues. Andy settled in Bend, OR which serves as his base of operations for national consulting operations.

"The simplest solution is the best solution." - Andy's derivative of Occam's Razor

Everyone has their own way of doing things. I'm always looking for the "right" way. That isn't always the popular choice. I would rather "get it right" than to be right. I'm poised to set the world on fire. I've been burnt along the way, but that just builds character. Don't you think?

I'm a property and casualty (P&C) claims expert, licensed property adjuster and Xactimate professional. I have served as an expert witness and appraiser in contractor disputes and insurance claim arbitration situations. My favorite thing is public speaking and education. I love to teach and inspire folks to be their best.

LinkedIn - www.linkedin.com/in/andymccabe

Website - www.claimsdelegates.com

Andrew McCabe has been a guest on The DYOJO Podcast Episode 5 and 37 (Pro vs. Joe 009)

Nunery II, Leroy, Dr.

Founder & Principal, PlūsUltré LLC

PlūsUltré LLC Background and Qualifications
PlūsUltré's mantra of "Inspiration. Imagination. Innovation" reflects our approach to enhancing the strategic and operational capacities of educational, non-profit, and entrepreneurial entities. Our breadth of experience and competence is demonstrated through inspired, objective, and creative problem-solving. Our clients engage us because we think and act objectively and critically, and with their interests in mind.

Turnaround and Transformation Expertise
Provide support, guidance and insight to get an organization "on track"
Bring actual performance in line with organizational mission and expectations
Planning for leadership transitions, process management, and redesign of workflows

Growth and Replication Expertise
Developing new business models based on value propositions, market analysis, and modeling
Evaluation and operation of educational business models: CMOs, EMOs, private/independent schools, and Higher Education
Provide Subject matter Expertise to educational technology companies and "disruptors" in the education space

Robust Network of Subject Matter Experts
Affiliation with deeply experienced practitioners in all areas of school/district/institutional operations and administration

Board Training and Consultation
Optimizing effectiveness and compliance
Board member recruitment and selection
Governance training

LinkedIn - www.linkedin.com/in/ldn2educate

Website - www.plusultrellc.net

Pasmanick, Elan

Mobile Equipment Repairs, Born to Repair

My mission is to transition the damage restoration industry to inhouse equipment repairs. Providing mobile equipment repairs for water damage equipment such as air movers and dehumidifiers. Born to Repair is also able to provide phone and video consulting to assist people outside of his service area. Elan is preparing an online repairs seminar as well.

Website - www.facebook.com/borntorepairsd

Check out Elan Pasmanick's water damage equipment maintenance and repair Tip of the Week as a regular feature on The DYOJO Podcast.

Princeton, David

Principle Consultant, Advocate Claim Service

Specializing in Contract Analysis & Risk Management.

Results-focused strategist with 16+ years of progressive career growth in the Insurance and Risk Management field. Tenaciously persistent in determining and attaining optimal outcomes. Astute negotiator. Background includes value-added, comprehensive expertise in analyzing insurance contracts, claim practices, and managing complex claims.

Advocate Claim Service was founded to provide policyholders

with a dedicated claim professional to develop a comprehensive claim presentation strategy. While ACS does not sell insurance, we do make it work for you. ACS's Principle Consultant, David Princeton, has resolved disputed claims resulting in total resolutions in excess of $25,000,000.

Specializing in the strategic presentation of claims, Advocate Claim Services looks to aid businesses in the presentation and resolution of doubtful and disputed claims. Our brand of advocacy focuses on the challenging claims that threaten to disrupt our clients' ability to do business.

LinkedIn - www.linkedin.com/in/davidrprinceton

Website - www.advocateclaimservice.com

David Princeton was a guest on The DYOJO Podcast Episode 1, 32 and 35 (Pro vs. Joe 007 and 008)

Stanley, Chris

Founder, IA Path

Author, *Independent Adjuster's Playbook* (and many more)

We help new adjusters get to work in 90 days with our online adjuster mentorships.

Most new adjusters struggle to meet hiring companies' experience requirements and have no way of getting started. At IA

Path we created a mentorship program that gets the experience requirements waived with over 20 companies so you can start working in the next 90 days.

LinkedIn - www.linkedin.com/in/iapath

Website - www.iapath.com

Chris Stanley was a guest on The DYOJO Podcast Episode 38

Watkin, Jeremy

Director of Customer Experience and Support, NumberBarn

Proven visionary leader, seasoned manager, and lifelong learner experienced in building both customer service teams and customer experience programs. Capable of creating a customer service operation from scratch and technically savvy enough to scale it with a rapidly growing business.

Top 50 Thought Leaders of 2017

Top 25 Thought Leaders in Technical Support and Service Management

Top 50 Thought Leaders to Follow on Twitter

Top 100 Customer Success Influencer

Vcare Top 50 Customer Care Influencer

ICMI's Top 50 Thought Leaders of 2015

Top 100 Customer Success Influencer

Top 50 Contact Center Thought Leaders on Twitter

Top 100 Most Social Customer Service Pros On Twitter

100 Most Influential Customer Service Twitter Accounts

LinkedIn - www.linkedin.com/in/jtwatkin

Website - www.customerservicelife.com

Jeremy Watkin was a guest on The DYOJO Podcast Episode 42

FOOTNOTES

[1] Isaacson, Jonathan L. (2020) *Be Intentional: Estimating.* The DYOJO. Pg. 17

[2] The DYOJO Podcast Episode 19

[3] The DYOJO Podcast Episode 39

[4] Sheridan, Richard (2013) *Joy, Inc. How We Built A Workplace People Love.* Penguin

[5] Isaacson, Jon (2018) Insurance Nerds. *The Four Keys to Developing a Well-Rounded Growth Mindset from MLK.* https://insnerds.com/four-keys-to-developing-a-well-rounded-growth-mindset-from-mlk/

[6] Luke 16:10

[7] Isaacson, Jonathan L. (2020) *Be Intentional: Estimating.* The DYOJO. Pg. 48-52

[8] Wickman, Gino. (2011) BenBella Books, Inc. *Traction: Get a Grip on Your Business.* Pg. 100

[9] Arcade Wayfinding. (2020, September 18). *Sink or Swim* (Episode 69). The Critical Path Podcast. https://www.arcadewayfinding.com/2020/09/18/episode-69-sink-or-swim/

[10] Sisney, Lex. (2012, February 20) *The Universal Success Formula.* https://or-

ganizationalphysics.com/2012/02/20/the-universal-success-formula/

[11] The DYOJO Podcast Episode 22

[12] Sisney, Lex. (2014, June 29) *The Culture System: Or, How to Integrate Your Values in Your Company.* OrganizationalPhysics.com. https://organizational-physics.com/2014/06/29/the-culture-system/

[13] Babin, Leif and Wilinik, Jocko. (2015) *Extreme Ownership: How U.S. Navy Seals Lead and Win.* St. Martin's Publishing Group.

[14] Denis Beaulieu joined us for The DYOJO Podcast Episode 15

[15] https://www.marsh.com/us/insights/research/the-journey-of-african-american-insurance-professionals.html

[16] www.nfl.com

[17] https://www.fastcompany.com/90407174/diversity-advertising-good-brands-bottom-line

[18] https://www.ceoaction.com/about

[19] https://fivethirtyeight.com/features/the-rooney-rule-isnt-working-anymore

[20] https://infokf.kornferry.com/The-Black-PandL-Leader-Report.html

[21] https://www.americanbar.org/groups/litigation/committees/insurance-coverage/articles/2019/diversity-inclusion-in-insurance-industry/

[22] https://thehill.com/policy/healthcare/346982-mylan-paying-465m-to-settle-claims-it-overcharged-for-epipens

[23] https://www.forbes.com/sites/jackkelly/2020/02/24/wells-fargo-forced-to-pay-3-billion-for-the-banks-fake-account-scandal/?sh=1a91093742d2

[24] Biography.com Editors (2014, April 2) *Les Paul Biography.* Biography.com. https://www.biography.com/musician/les-paul

[25] Bright, Kimberly. (2016, August 17) *Kalamazoo Gals: The Secret Behind Gibson's WWII Guitars.* She Shreds. https://sheshreds.com/the-kalamazoo-gals/

[26] Imperial War Museums Editors. *The Workers that kept Britain Going During the Second World War.* IWM. https://www.iwm.org.uk/history/the-workers-that-kept-britain-going-during-the-second-world-war

[27] Blevins, Michelle (2016, October 25) *Recognizing Women in Restoration: 2016 The Best of the Best.* Restoration and Remediation Magazine. https://www.randrmagonline.com/articles/87090-recognizing-women-in-restoration-2016-best-of-the-best

[28] The DYOJO Podcast Episode 25

[29] https://kickasscareers.org/about - Shannon Tymosko, aka Lady Voltz, was a guest on The DYOJO Podcast Episode 39

[30] Thurber, Jon. (2001, April 8) *Theodore McCarty; Key Figure in Electric Guitar's Development.* Los Angeles Times. https://www.latimes.com/archives/la-xpm-2001-apr-08-me-48572-story.html

[31] Price, Huw. (2018, June 4) *All About...Ted McCarty.* Guitar.com https://gui-

tar.com/guides/essential-guide/ted-mccarty/

[32] If you want to hear more about these experiences and a funny story about *this* manager, listen to The DYOJO Podcast Episode 15

[33] Yellen, Sheldon. (2019, March 16) *What Undercover Boss Taught Me About Being A Better Leader*. Score. https://www.score.org/blog/what-undercover-boss-taught-me-about-being-better-leader

[34] The DYOJO Podcast Episode 9

[35] Sisney, Lex. (2017) *The 3 Covenants*. Organizational Physics. https://organizationalphysics.com/wp-content/uploads/Organizational-Physics-The-3-Covenants.pdf

[36] The DYOJO Podcast Episode 31

[37] Carlozo, Lou. (2017, December 6) *How This Man Made $27 Million From His $3,000 Business*. The Huffington Post. https://www.huffpost.com/entry/how-this-man-made-27-mill_b_7795676

[38] www.thedyojo.com/dogood

[39] https://www.randrmagonline.com/articles/86958-peeling-back-5-layers-of-communication-in-a-restoration-business

[40] https://www.randrmagonline.com/articles/89124-nothing-is-scarier-than-scope-creep